President Ronald Reagan warned, "freedom is never more than one generation away from extinction." Mark R. Levin agrees and, in exposing the forces eroding our nation's founding principles, "gets to the core of what drives not just the American Left in the Obama era but what has driven left-wingers through the millennia of human existence itself: Utopia."*

FROM THE AUTHOR OF *LIBERTY AND TYRANNY*

Praise for Mark R. Levin's #1 *New York Times* bestseller

AMERITOPIA

"This book is going to be a classic. One day some society will look at this and make it a foundation. It's that powerful."

—Sean Hannity

"The companion book to *Liberty and Tyranny*. . . . Levin's analysis is deadly to liberalism. . . . *Ameritopia* is historical X-ray vision in book form."

—Jeffrey Lord, *The American Spectator**

"A must-read for Americans of all political persuasions. . . . An honest discussion of the dangers presently facing our country. . . . Levin does a fantastic job."

—Jedediah Bila, *Newsmax*

"Mark Levin has a unique ability to take complex subjects and boil them down to their essentials."

—Erick Erickson, *Red State*

"Eye-opening. . . . Levin demonstrates that what most threatens America today is a thought process and a mindset that deserve a front-row seat on the ash heap of history. . . . A fast-moving conversation that you need to have."

—C. Edmund Wright, *American Thinker*

"I don't have to write another book because Mark Levin wrote *Ameritopia*."

—**Rush Limbaugh**

"Reminiscent of Whittaker Chambers's melancholy assessment in *Witness* that his renunciation of Communism amounted to joining the losing side, Levin ruefully observes that 'Ameritopia'—the term he coins for the overrunning of our freedom culture by the Progressives' utopian project—is not some distant prospect. Ameritopia is here. . . . The stark question Mark Levin poses is whether we are so far gone that the losses are permanent. Do we throw off Ameritopia and pivot back toward liberty and self-determination? Or will we remember this pass as 'the good old days,' the soft tyranny in an inexorable disintegration into some harsher variety that has, for millennia, been the fate of failed democracies? Levin—insightful, fact-driven, pulling no punches—characteristically declines to don rose-tinted glasses. *Ameritopia* is the deep contemplation of a staunch believer in the vision of the American founding, one who sees that if dramatic counteraction does not begin promptly, all will be lost. The chilling part is that he is anything but sanguine about the likely outcome."

—**Andrew C. McCarthy,** *The New Criterion*

"Few modern books direct our attention to first principles. *Ameritopia* examines more deeply the historical and philosophical roots of the utopian ideal, for it is that ideal that has always animated the liberal worldview."

—**David Limbaugh,** *Town Hall*

"A history lesson, a philosophical treatise, and a political science lesson. Levin examine[s] the fundamental foundations of today's politics . . . with his lawyerly precision."

—*The Denver Post*

"That Levin wrote this book now demonstrates not only his passion for the United States, but his awareness that he is a statesman defending natural law at a pivotal moment in human history. . . . Mark Levin [does] the lion's share of our shouting—eloquently—with *Ameritopia*."

—*PJ Media*

The astounding *New York Times* bestseller that held the #1 spot for twelve weeks . . . more than one million copies sold! Mark R. Levin's conservative manifesto

LIBERTY AND TYRANNY

"The necessary book of the Obama era."

—**Jeffrey Lord,** *The American Spectator*

"The most compelling defense of freedom for our time."

—**Rush Limbaugh**

"Simply spectacular. If you love this country, read it. And then thank Mark Levin."

—**Sean Hannity**

"Empowering, captivating, and enlightening. . . . A testament to both the potential grandeur and potential extinction of this great country as we know it."

—**Jedediah Bila,** *Conservative Examiner*

"Timely yet timeless. . . . *Liberty and Tyranny* couldn't be more relevant."

—**David Limbaugh,** *Town Hall*

"This is quite simply the most important book of our times."

—**Scott Miller,** *The Conservative Post*

AMERITOPIA

THE UNMAKING OF AMERICA

Mark R. Levin

THRESHOLD EDITIONS

New York London Toronto Sydney New Delhi

Threshold Editions
A Division of Simon & Schuster, Inc.
1230 Avenue of the Americas
New York, NY 10020

First Threshold Editions paperback edition September 2012

THRESHOLD EDITIONS and colophon are trademarks of
Simon & Schuster, Inc.

For information about special discounts for bulk purchases,
please contact Simon & Schuster Special Sales at 1-866-506-1949
or business@simonandschuster.com.

The Simon & Schuster Speakers Bureau can bring authors
to your live event. For more information or to book an event,
contact the Simon & Schuster Speakers Bureau at 1-866-248-3049
or visit our website at www.simonspeakers.com.

Designed by Joy O'Meara

Manufactured in the United States of America

10   9   8   7   6   5   4   3

Library of Congress Cataloging-in-Publication Data

Levin, Mark R. (Mark Reed), 1957–
    Ameritopia : the unmaking of America / Mark R. Levin.
        p.   cm.
    1. United States—Politics and government—Philosophy.   2. Democracy—
United States.   3. Utopias—United States.   4. Utopias—
Philosophy.   I. Title.
    JK31.L47 2012
    320.97301—dc23   2011042260

ISBN 978-1-4391-7324-4
ISBN 978-1-4391-7327-5 (pbk)
ISBN 978-1-4391-7328-2 (ebook)

To my beloved family

CONTENTS

ix

CONTENTS

INTRODUCTION

IN *LIBERTY AND TYRANNY,* I described the nature of individual liberty and the civil society in a constitutional republic, including the essential principles of America's societal and political order. I also discussed the growing tyranny of government—statism, as I broadly labeled it—which threatens our liberty, the character of our country, and our way of life. At the time I warned that if we do not come to grips with the significance of this transformation, we will be devoured by it.

The symptoms of the tyranny that threatens liberty and republicanism have been acknowledged throughout time, including by iconic Americans. For example, Supreme Court associate justice Joseph Story, among America's most prominent legal thinkers, explained in 1829, "governments are not always overthrown by direct and open assaults. They are not always battered down by the arms of conquerors, or the successful daring of usurpers. There is often concealed the dry rot, which eats into the vitals, when all is fair and stately on the outside. And to republics this has been the more common fatal disease. The continual drippings of corruption may wear away the solid rock, when the tempest has failed to overturn it. . . ."[1]

In 1838, Abraham Lincoln delivered an address before the Young Men's Lyceum of Springfield, Illinois. He declared, "At what point . . . is the approach of danger to be expected. I answer, If it ever reach us it must spring up amongst us; it cannot come from abroad. If destruction be our lot we must ourselves be its author and finisher. As a nation of freemen we must live through all time, or die by suicide."[2]

In this same vein, for years President Ronald Reagan cautioned that "[f]reedom is never more than one generation away from extinction. We didn't pass it to our children in the bloodstream. It must be fought for, protected, and handed on for them to do the same, or one day we will spend our sunset years telling our children and our children's children what it was once like in the United States where men were free."[3]

During the three years since the publication of *Liberty and Tyranny*, and despite growing alarm by an increasingly alert segment of the public, too many of our fellow citizens remain oblivious to the perilousness of their surroundings, not realizing or accepting the precariousness of their liberty and the civil society in the face of the federal government's dramatic, albeit predictable, engorgement of power. This is the grave reality of our day.

But what is this ideology, this force, this authority that threatens us, and its destructiveness, which Reagan, Lincoln, Story, and the Founders so feared? What kind of power both attracts a free people and destroys them?

The mission of this book is to delve deeper into these essential questions, the most important of our time, and identify, expose, and explain the character of the threat that America and, indeed, all republics confront. In this way we can better comprehend the existential danger to a free and prosperous people.

In *Ameritopia*, I explain that the heart of the problem is, in fact, utopianism, a term I discuss in great detail throughout the book. Utopianism is the ideological and doctrinal foundation for statism. While *utopianism* and *statism* or *utopian* and *statist* are often used interchangeably, the undertaking here is to probe more deeply into what motivates and animates the tyranny of statism. Indeed, the modern arguments about the necessities and virtues of government control over the individual are but malign echoes of utopian prescriptions through the ages, which attempted to define subjugation as the most transcendent state of man.

Utopianism has long promoted the idea of a paradisiacal existence and advanced concepts of pseudo "ideal" societies in which a heroic despot, a benevolent sovereign, or an enlightened oligarchy claims the ability and authority to provide for all the needs and fulfill all the wants of the individual—in exchange for his abject servitude.

By sorting through an immense volume of writings, I chose those books and passages—using the original words of certain classic philosophical works—that best describe the utopian mind-set and its application to modern-day utopian thinking and conduct in America. Plato's *Republic*, Thomas More's *Utopia*, Thomas Hobbes's *Leviathan*, and Karl Marx's *Communist Manifesto* are indispensable in understanding the nature of utopianism. They are essential works that have in common soulless societies in which the individual is subsumed into a miasma of despotism—and each of them is a warning against utopian transformation in America and elsewhere.

I also contrast the utopian societies created by these writings with the enlightened thinking of philosophical pioneers John Locke and Charles de Montesquieu, among others, who described truisms about the nature of man—liberty, rights, and life—that informed the Founders and became the touchstone of American society. Indeed, their wisdom served as the bone and sinew of the Declaration of Independence and the Constitution.

Moreover, a proper examination of democracy's tendency to descend into a soft tyranny or worse would be incomplete without Alexis de Tocqueville's prescient insight. Although not a contemporary of the Founders, he wrote elaborately about the unique character of the American people and their government, praising them but also drawing attention to the historical weaknesses of democratic institutions and to the fragility of liberty.

I also endeavor to show how insidiously contemporary utopians or statists have poisoned modern society by changing the paradigms under which governmental action is both contemplated and executed. For example, we seldom question today whether it is appropriate for the federal government to undertake a given task, no matter how significant or minute. In infinite ways, whether we realize it or not, this is the utopian mind-set at work.

Finally, there is a reflexive desire when concluding a project such as this to put a positive spin on the situation. I have not done so here. I remain convinced that we, the people, are at great risk. There simply are no easy answers to the challenges we face. It will take nothing short of a prodigious effort, of the kind I discussed in *Liberty and Tyranny*, over a course of many decades, to reestablish America as a constitutional republic. However, this is an effort we must make, no matter how complicated and daunting. Otherwise, as Lincoln put it, the nation will surely "die by suicide."

I believe the provenance of liberty and tyranny matters. To know liberty is to cherish it. Conversely, utopianism is tyranny born of intellectual bankruptcy and dishonesty. The proof is seen every day in the words and actions of politicians, judges, bureaucrats, and the media. It is my hope that, in some small way, this book will contribute to a broader awakening of the citizenry and the reaffirmation and reestablishment of the principles that secure and nurture individual liberty, inalienable rights, the civil society, and constitutional republicanism.

Mark R. Levin

PART I

ON UTOPIANISM

CHAPTER ONE

———————————

THE TYRANNY OF UTOPIA

TYRANNY, BROADLY DEFINED, IS the use of power to dehumanize the individual and delegitimize his nature. Political utopianism[1] is tyranny disguised as a desirable, workable, and even paradisiacal governing ideology. There are, of course, unlimited utopian constructs, for the mind is capable of infinite fantasies. But there are common themes. The fantasies take the form of grand social plans or experiments, the impracticability and impossibility of which, in small ways and large, lead to the individual's subjugation.

Karl Popper, a philosopher who eloquently deconstructed the false assumptions and scientific claims of utopianism, arguing it is totalitarian in form and substance, observed that "[a]ny social science which does not teach the impossibility of rational social

construction is entirely blind to the most important facts of social
life, and must overlook the only social laws of real validity and of
real importance. Social sciences seeking to provide a background
for social engineering cannot, therefore, be true descriptions of
social facts. They are impossible in themselves."[2] Popper argued
that unable to make detailed or precise sociological predictions,
long-term forecasts of great sweep and significance not only are
intended to compensate for utopianism's shortcomings but are the
only forecasts it considers worth pursuing.[3] (Although Popper differentiated between "piecemeal social engineering" and "utopian
social engineering," it is ahistorical, or at least a leap of faith, to
suggest that once unleashed, the social engineers will not become
addicted to their power; and Popper never could enunciate a practical solution.)

Utopianism is irrational in theory and practice, for it ignores or
attempts to control the planned and unplanned complexity of the
individual, his nature, and mankind generally. It ignores, rejects,
or perverts the teachings and knowledge that have come before—
that is, man's historical, cultural, and social experience and development. Indeed, utopianism seeks to break what the hugely
influential eighteenth-century British statesman and philosopher
Edmund Burke argued was the societal continuum "between those
who are living and those who are dead and those who are to be
born."[4] Eric Hoffer, a social thinker renowned for his observations about fanaticism and mass movements, commented that
"[f]or men to plunge headlong into an undertaking of vast change,
they must be intensely discontented yet not destitute, and they
must have the feeling that by the possession of some potent doctrine, infallible leader or some new technique they have access to

a source of irresistible power. They must also have an extravagant conception of the prospects and potentialities of the future. . . . [T]hey must be wholly ignorant of the difficulties involved in their vast undertaking. Experience is a handicap."[5]

Utopianism substitutes glorious predictions and unachievable promises for knowledge, science, and reason, while laying claim to them all. Yet there is nothing new in deception disguised as hope and nothing original in abstraction framed as progress. A heavenly society is said to be within reach if only the individual surrenders more of his liberty and being for the general good, meaning the good as prescribed by the state. If he refuses, he will be tormented and ultimately coerced into compliance, for conformity is essential. Indeed, nothing good can come of self-interest, which is condemned as morally indefensible and empty. Through persuasion, deceit, and coercion, the individual must be stripped of his identity and subordinated to the state. He must abandon his own ambitions for the ambitions of the state. He must become reliant on and fearful of the state. His first duty must be to the state—not family, community, and faith, all of which challenge the authority of the state. Once dispirited, the individual can be molded by the state with endless social experiments and lifestyle calibrations.[6]

Especially threatening, therefore, are the industrious, independent, and successful, for they demonstrate what is actually possible under current societal conditions—achievement, happiness, and fulfillment—thereby contradicting and endangering the utopian campaign against what was or is. They must be either co-opted and turned into useful contributors to or advocates for the state, or neutralized through sabotage or other means. Indeed, the individual's contribution to society must be downplayed, dismissed, or denounced, unless the contribution is directed by the state and involves self-sacrifice for the utopian cause.

In a somewhat different context, although relatable here, the extraordinary French historian and prescient political thinker Alexis de Tocqueville explained, "When the traces of individual action upon nations are lost, it often happens that you see the world move without the impelling force being evident. As it becomes extremely difficult to discern and analyze the reasons that, acting separately on the will of each member of the community, concur in the end to produce movement in the whole mass, men are led to believe that his movement is involuntary and that societies unconsciously obey some superior force ruling over them. But even when the general fact that governs the private volition of all individuals is supposed to be discovered upon the earth, the principle of human free-will is not made certain. A cause sufficiently extensive to affect millions of men at once and sufficiently strong to bend them all together in the same direction may well seem irresistible, having seen that mankind do yield to it, the mind is close upon the inference that mankind cannot resist it."[7] Tocqueville was writing of religion but his observation assuredly applies to utopian tyranny.

Utopianism also attempts to shape and dominate the individual by doing two things at once: it strips the individual of his uniqueness, making him indistinguishable from the multitudes that form what is commonly referred to as "the masses," but it simultaneously assigns him a group identity based on race, ethnicity, age, gender, income, etc., to highlight differences within the masses. It then exacerbates old rivalries and disputes or it incites new ones. This way it can speak to the well-being of "the people" as a whole while dividing them against themselves, thereby stampeding them in one direction or another as necessary to collapse the existing society or rule over the new one.

Where utopianism is advanced through gradualism rather than revolution, albeit steady and persistent as in democratic societies, it can deceive and disarm an unsuspecting population, which is largely content and passive. It is sold as reforming and improving the existing society's imperfections and weaknesses without imperiling its basic nature. Under these conditions, it is mostly ignored, dismissed, or tolerated by much of the citizenry and celebrated by some. Transformation is deemed innocuous, well-intentioned, and perhaps constructive but not a dangerous trespass on fundamental liberties. Tocqueville observed, "By this system the people shake off their state of dependence just long enough to select their master and then relapse into it again. A great many persons . . . are quite contented with this sort of compromise between administrative despotism and the sovereignty of the people; and they think they have done enough for the protection of individual freedom when they have surrendered it to the power of the nation at large . . ." (II, 319)

Utopianism also finds a receptive audience among the society's disenchanted, disaffected, dissatisfied, and maladjusted who are unwilling or unable to assume responsibility for their own real or perceived conditions but instead blame their surroundings, "the system," and others. They are lured by the false hopes and promises of utopian transformation and the criticisms of the existing society, to which their connection is tentative or nonexistent. Improving the malcontent's lot becomes linked to the utopian cause. Moreover, disparaging and diminishing the successful and accomplished becomes an essential tactic. No one should be better than anyone else, regardless of the merits or value of his contributions. By exploiting human frailties, frustrations, jealousies, and inequities, a sense of meaning and self-worth is created in the malcontent's otherwise unhappy and directionless life. Simply put, equality in misery—that is, equality of result or conformity—is advanced as a just, fair, and virtuous undertaking. Liberty, therefore, is inherently immoral, except where it avails equality.

Equality, in this sense, is a form of radical egalitarianism that has long been the subject of grave concern by advocates of liberty. Tocqueville pointed out that in democracies, the dangers of misapplied equality are not perceived until it is too late. "The evils that extreme equality may produce are slowly disclosed; they creep gradually into the social frame; they are seen only at intervals; and at the moment at which they become most violent, habit already causes them to be no longer felt"[8] (II, 319). Among the leading classical liberal philosophers and free-market economists, Friedrich Hayek wrote, "Equality of the general rules of law and conduct . . . is the only kind of equality conducive to liberty and the only equality which we can secure without destroying liberty. Not only has liberty nothing to do with any sort of equality, but it is even bound to produce inequality in many respects. This is the necessary result and part of the justification of individual liberty: if the result of individual liberty did not demonstrate that some manners of living are more successful than others, much of the case for it would vanish."[9] Thus, while radical egalitarianism encompasses economic equality, it more broadly involves prostrating the individual.

Equality, as understood by the American Founders, is the natural right of every individual to live freely under self-government, to acquire and retain the property he creates through his own labor, and to be treated impartially before a just law. Moreover, equality should not be confused with perfection, for man is also imperfect, making his application of equality, even in the most just society, imperfect. Otherwise, inequality is the natural state of man in the sense that each individual is born unique in all his human characteristics. Therefore, equality and inequality, properly comprehended, are both engines of liberty.[10]

Still, in democracies, the attraction of equality too often outweighs the appeal of liberty, even though individuals are able to flourish more in democracies than in other societies. Liberty's wonders and permeance can be subtle and ambiguous and, therefore, unnoticed and underappreciated. Despite its infinite benefits, for many liberty is elusive—for one must look below the surface to identify it. Conversely, equality can be more transparent at surface level. It is posited as a far-off concept of human perfectibility but is also delivered in bits and pieces, or at least appears to be, in daily life. It usually takes the form of material "rights" delivered to the individual by the state. Consequently, equality and liberty are both subjects of utopian demagoguery and manipulation. Liberty is encouraged if its end is equality. Liberty, by itself, is not.

Equality is also disguised as or confused with popular sovereignty—that is, the conflation of "the people's will" with egalitarian campaigns, such as "social justice," "environmental justice," "immigrant rights," "workers' rights," etc. In essence, then, true democracy cannot be achieved unless society is reorganized around the disparate and endless demands of disparate and endless claimants. In due course, such a society becomes chaotic and balkanized. As it dissolves and crises build, the stage is set for escalating coercion or repression.

Utopianism's authority also knows no definable limits. How could it? If they exist, what are they? Radical egalitarianism or the perfectibility of mankind is an ongoing process of individual and societal transformation that must cast off the limits of history, tradition, and experience for that which is said to be necessary, novel, progressive, and inevitable. Ironically, inconvenient facts and evidence must be rejected or manipulated, as must the very nature of man, for utopianism is a fantasy that evolves into a dogmatic cause, which, in turn, manifests a holy truth for a false religion. There is little or no tolerance for the individual's deviation from orthodoxy lest it threaten the survival of the enterprise.

In truth, therefore, utopianism is regressive, irrational, and pre-Enlightenment. It robs society of opinions and ideas that may be beneficial to the human condition, now and in the future. It stymies human interaction, including economic activity, which progresses through a historical process of self-organization. Adam Smith, a towering philosopher and economist of the Scottish Enlightenment, referred to it as a harmony of interests creating a spontaneous order where rules of cooperation have developed through generations of human experience,[11] The utopian pursuit, however, commands the imposition of a purported design and structure atop society by a central authority to arrest the evolution of the individual and society.

As Popper noted, "[T]he power of the state is bound to increase until the State becomes nearly identical with society. . . . It is the totalitarian intuition. . . . The term 'society' embraces . . . all social relations, including all personal ones."[12] The power, according to Tocqueville, is "immense and tutelary" and "takes upon itself alone to secure" the people's "gratifications and watch over their fate." "That power is absolute, minute, regular, provident, and mild." "Thus it every day renders the exercise of the free agency of man less useful and less frequent; it circumscribes the will within a narrower range and gradually robs a man of all the uses of himself." "It covers the surface of society with a network of small complicated rules, minute and uniform, through which the most original minds and the most energetic characters cannot penetrate, to rise above the crowd." (II, 318)

Utopianism's equality is intolerant of diversity, uniqueness, debate, etc., for utopianism's purpose requires a singular focus. There can be no competing voices or causes slowing or obstructing society's long and righteous march. Utopianism relies on deceit, propaganda, dependence, intimidation, and force. In its more aggressive state, as the malignancy of the enterprise becomes more painful and its impossibility more obvious, it incites violence inasmuch as avenues for free expression and civil dissent are cut off. Violence becomes the individual's primary recourse and the state's primary response. Ultimately, the only way out is the state's termination.[13]

In utopia, rule by masterminds is both necessary and necessarily primitive, for it excludes so much that is known to man and about man. The mastermind is driven by his own boundless conceit and delusional aspirations, which he self-identifies as a noble calling. He alone is uniquely qualified to carry out this mission. He is, in his own mind, a savior of mankind, if only man will bend to his will. Such can be the addiction of power. It can be an irrationally egoistic and absurdly frivolous passion that engulfs even sensible people. In this, the mastermind suffers from a psychosis of sorts and endeavors to substitute his own ambitions for the individual ambitions of millions of people.

Legislatures are capable of democratic tyranny by degenerating into a collection of masterminds, passing laws not because they are right or moral, but because they can. Writing of the French Legislative Assembly, Frédéric Bastiat, a statesman and pioneering advocate of classical liberalism, noted, "It is indeed fortunate that Heaven has bestowed upon certain men—governors and legislators—the exact opposite inclinations, not only for their own sake but also for the sake of the rest of the world! While mankind tends toward evil, the legislators yearn for good; while mankind advances toward darkness, the legislators aspire for enlightenment; while mankind is drawn toward vice, the legislators are attracted toward virtue. Since they have decided that this is the true state of affairs, they then demand the use of force in order to substitute their own inclinations for those of the human race." He added that there "is this idea that mankind is merely inert matter, receiving life, organization, morality, and prosperity from the power of the state. And even worse, it will be stated that mankind tends toward degeneration, and is stopped from this downward course only by the mysterious hand of the legislator."[14] Thomas Jefferson put it this way: "All the powers of government, legislative, executive, and judiciary, result to the legislative body. The concentrating of these in the same hands is precisely the definition of despotic government. It will be no alleviation that these powers will be exercised by a plurality of hands, and not by a single one. One hundred and seventy-three despots would surely be as oppressive as one . . . As little will it avail us that they are chosen by ourselves. An *elective despotism* was not the government we fought for. . . ."[15]

The mastermind is served by an enthusiastic intelligentsia or "experts" professionally engaged in developing and spreading utopian fantasies. Although there are conspicuous exceptions, longtime Harvard professor and political theoretician Harvey Mansfield explained that modern intellectuals have "monumental impatience . . . with human complexity and imperfection. . . . They believe that politics is a temporary necessity until the rational solution is put in place."[16] Of course, the rational solutions are not rational at all. While intellectuals are obviously smart, they are not smart enough to have conquered the social sciences and use them to rejigger society. They are posers to knowledge they do not and cannot possess. Meanwhile, intellectuals are immune from the impracticability and consequences of their blueprints for they rarely present themselves for public office. Instead, they seek to influence those who do. They legislate without accountability. Joseph Schumpeter, a prominent economics professor and political scientist, was a harsh critic of intellectuals. He wrote, "Intellectuals rarely enter professional politics and still more rarely conquer responsible office. But they staff political bureaus, write party pamphlets and speeches, act as secretaries and advisers, make the . . . politician's . . . reputation. . . . In doing these things they . . . impress their mentality on almost everything that is being done."[17]

For the rest, transforming society becomes a struggle between the utopia and self-determination and self-preservation, since the individual must acquiesce to centralized decision-making. Apart from brute force, the mastermind has in his arsenal a weapon that provides him with a predominant advantage—the law. Bastiat explained that "when [the law] has exceeded its proper functions, it has not done so merely in some inconsequential and debatable matters. The law has gone further than this; it has acted in direct opposition to its own proper purpose. The law has been used to destroy its own objective: It has been applied to annihilating the justice that it was supposed to maintain; to limiting and destroying rights which its real appeal was to respect. The law has placed the collective force at the disposal of the unscrupulous who wish, without risk, to exploit the person, liberty, and property of others. It has converted plunder into a right, in order to protect plunder. And it has converted lawful defense into a crime, in order to punish lawful defense."[18] When the law is used in this way, the few plunder the many (e.g., public-sector unions), the many plunder the few (e.g., the progressive income tax), and everyone plunders everyone (e.g., universal health care), making utopia unsustainable and ultimately inhumane.

Centralizing and consolidating authority is required to replace dispersed decision-making with a command and control structure, the purpose of which is to coerce behavior in pursuit of a fantasy, a dogmatic cause, a false religion, etc. That is not to say that knowledge and information from outside the central authority go without notice. Rather, it is collected in a self-serving, haphazard, and incomplete way, to tinker and adjust, to torment and control, but never as a means to fundamentally challenge assumptions, reconsider policies, or disprove the utopian ends. How could it, since utopianism rejects rationality and empiricism from the outset? It repudiates experience. It is said to be new, different, better, and bigger.

Moreover, the reproduction of knowledge and information that exists outside the central authority would be not only pointless but impossible. Individuals are complicated, complex beings. No centralized authority can know what is in their minds or discern and assimilate the distinctiveness and assortment of their myriad daily activities, no matter how many academics or experts advise it. For example, respecting the social engineers and their distortion of economics to justify their manipulation of behavior and outcomes, Popper noted, "Economics . . . cannot give us any valuable information concerning social reforms. Only a pseudo-economics can seek to offer a background for rational understanding."[19]

Consequently, the mastermind relies on uniform standards born of insufficient knowledge and information, which are crafted from his own predilections, values, stereotypes, experiences, idiosyncrasies, desires, prejudices and, of course, fantasy. The imposition of these standards may, in the short term, benefit some or perhaps many. But over time, the misery and corrosiveness from their full effects spread through the whole of society. Although the mastermind's incompetence and vision plague the society, responsibility must be diverted elsewhere—to those assigned to carry them out, or to the people's lack of sacrifice, or to the enemies of the state who have conspired to thwart the utopian cause—for the mastermind is inextricably linked to the fantasy. If he is fallible then who is to usher in paradise? If his judgment and wisdom are in doubt then the entire venture might invite scrutiny. This leads to grander and bolder social experiments, requiring further coercion. What went before is said to have been piecemeal and therefore inadequate. The steps necessary to achieve true utopianism have yet to be tried.

For the individual and the people generally, this is dispiriting, destabilizing, stagnating, and impoverishing. Although all state action is said to be taken in the people's interest, the heavy if not crippling burden they shoulder is the price they pay for an impossible cause—a cause greater than their lives, liberty, and happiness. The individual is inconsequential as a person and useful only as an insignificant part of an agglomeration of insignificant parts. He is a worker, part of a mass; nothing more, nothing less. His existence is soulless. Absolute obedience is the highest virtue. After all, only an army of drones is capable of building a rainbow to paradise.

The immorality of utopianism, albeit obvious to sober thinkers, requires explicit attention nonetheless for, perversely, too many remain enthusiastically committed to it. Utopianism is immoral per se. On what basis does utopianism make such a thorough claim on the individual's existence? On a mastermind's dogma? In criticizing socialism's immorality and its appeal to "dropouts" and "parasites," Hayek wrote, "Rights derive from systems of relations of which the claimant has become a part through helping to maintain them. If he ceases to do so, or has never done so (or nobody has done so for him) there exists no ground on which such claims could be forwarded. Relations between individuals can exist only as products of their wills, but the mere wish of a claimant can hardly create a duty for others. . . ."[20] More broadly, the individual's right to live freely and safely and pursue happiness includes the right to benefit from the fruits of his own labor. As the individual's time on earth is finite, so, too, is his labor. The illegitimate denial or diminution of his labor—that is, the involuntary deprivation of the private property he accumulates from his intellectual and/ or physical efforts—is a form of servitude and, hence, immoral.[21]

There is also no morality in utopian deception and distortion to promote an abstraction, forcing the individual to behave in ways that are contrary to his best interests and destructive of his nature; attacking the civil society's ethical norms and social arrangements; and making commonplace dependency and coercion. Rather than cultivating a moral society and individual virtuousness, whether through faith, education, or sociability, and building on the accumulated experience and wisdom of earlier generations, utopianism breeds dishonesty not good character; it encourages ideology not reason; it rewards rashness not reflection; it attracts fanatics not statesmen; and it is transformative not reformative. As the world around him grows increasingly unpredictable and hostile, and the moral order of the civil society frays and then unravels, the individual may feel that his daily survival depends on abandoning his own moral nature and teaching, including prudence, self-restraint, and forethought. He may become radicalized and join the ranks of predators, or become isolated and conniving, hoping to avoid notice. He may become dispirited and detached, resigned to a life of misery. He may defiantly stand his moral ground, in which case he may become the predators' prey. In any event, the law of the jungle becomes the law of the land as the civil society disintegrates.

Clearly, utopianism is incompatible with constitutionalism. Utopianism requires power to be concentrated in a central authority with maximum latitude to transform and control. Oppositely, a constitution establishes parameters that define the form and the limits of government. For example, in the United States, the Constitution divides, disperses, and delineates governmental power. It grants the central government not plenary but enumerated pow-

18 MARK R. LEVIN

ers. It further deconcentrates power through three branches of the central government, reserving the rest of governmental powers to the states and the people. The Constitution enshrines a governing framework intended to ensure the longevity of the existing society and stifle the potential for tyranny.

The Constitution reflects the Founders' repudiation of utopianism and any notion of omnipotent and omniscient masterminds. In *Federalist* 51, James Madison wrote, "But what is government itself but the greatest of all reflections on human nature? If men were angels, no government would be necessary. If angels were to govern men, neither external nor internal controls on government would be necessary. In framing a government which is to be administered by men over men, the great difficulty lies in this: you must first enable the government to control the governed; and in the next place oblige it to control itself."[22] Madison argued that the draft constitution had achieved that end. In *Federalist* 45, he explained, "The powers delegated by the proposed Constitution to the federal government are few and defined. Those which are to remain in the State governments are numerous and indefinite. The former will be exercised principally on external objects, as war, peace, negotiation, and foreign commerce; with which last the power of taxation will, for the most part, be connected. The powers reserved to the several States will extend to all the objects which, in the ordinary course of affairs, concern the lives, liberties, and properties of the people, and the internal order, improvement, and prosperity of the State."[23]

For the mastermind, where the Constitution is believed useful to utopian ends, it will be invoked. Where it is not, under the pretense of legitimate differences of interpretation it will be abandoned outright or remade through various doctrinal schemes and administrative evasions. For the mastermind, the Constitution's words are as undeserving of respect as the rest of history. They will be used to muddle and disarrange, not inform and clarify. Moreover, the Constitution's authors, ratifiers, and present-day proponents will be dismissed as throwbacks. To follow them will be to renounce modernity and progress. And yet to follow the mastermind is to renounce the American founding and heritage.

The late associate Supreme Court justice Thurgood Marshall demonstrated the point in his repudiation of the Framers. "I do not believe that the meaning of the Constitution was forever 'fixed' at the Philadelphia Convention. . . . Nor do I find the wisdom, foresight and sense of justice exhibited by the framers particularly profound. To the contrary, the government they devised was defective from the start, requiring several amendments, a civil war and momentous social transformation to attain the system of constitutional government, and its respect for the individual freedoms and human rights, we hold as fundamental today. They could not have imagined, nor would they have accepted, that the document they were drafting would one day be construed by a Supreme Court to which had been appointed a woman and the descendant of an African slave. 'We the people' no longer enslave, but the credit does not belong to the framers. It belongs to those who refused to acquiesce in outdated notions of 'liberty,' 'justice' and 'equality,' and who strived to better them." [24]

There is no denying that slavery blights the history of many societies, including American society. But the Constitution neither preserved nor promoted slavery. As I explained in my response to Marshall in *Men in Black,* "Discrimination, injustice, and inhumanity are not products of the Constitution. To the extent they exist, they result from man's imperfection. Consequently, slavery exists today not in the United States but in places like Sudan. Indeed, the evolution of American society has only been possible because of the covenant the framers adopted, and the values, ideals, and rules set forth in that document."[25] In fact, had there been no Constitution there would have been no United States. If there had been no United States there would have been no Civil War—no Union versus Confederacy. Slavery in the southern colonies and later the territories may well have lasted much longer. While the delegates to the Constitutional Convention were unable to abolish slavery, many tried. Moreover, their progeny did, and at great personal sacrifice.

The Constitution evinces the Founders' broader comprehension of human nature and natural rights, set forth most succinctly and prominently in the Declaration of Independence. To cast the Constitution off its mooring is to cast off its mooring as well. The Declaration provides, in part:

> When in the Course of human events, it becomes necessary for one people to dissolve the political bands which have connected them with another, and to assume among the powers of the earth, the separate and equal station to which the Laws of Nature and of Nature's God entitle them, a decent respect to the opinions of mankind requires that they should declare the causes which impel them to the separation. We hold these truths to be self-evident, that all men are created equal, that they are endowed by their Creator with certain unalienable Rights, that among these are Life, Liberty and the pursuit of Happiness.—

That to secure these rights, Governments are instituted among Men, deriving their just powers from the consent of the governed. . . .

President Abraham Lincoln, during his 1858 campaign for the U.S. Senate, explained: "In [the Founders'] enlightened belief, nothing stamped with the Divine image and likeness was sent into the world to be trodden on, and degraded, and imbruted by its fellows. They grasped not only the whole race of man then living, but they reached forward and seized upon the farthest posterity. They erected a beacon to guide their children and their children's children, and the countless myriads who should inhabit the earth in other ages. Wise statesmen as they were, they knew the tendency of prosperity to breed tyrants, and so they established these great self-evident truths, that when in the distant future some man, some faction, some interest, should set up the doctrine that none but rich men, or none but white men, were entitled to life, liberty and the pursuit of happiness, their posterity might look up again to the Declaration of Independence and take courage to renew the battle which their fathers began—so that truth, and justice, and mercy, and all the humane and Christian virtues might not be extinguished from the land; so that no man would hereafter dare to limit and circumscribe the great principles on which the temple of liberty was being built. . . ."[26]

America's founding documents set in place the philosophical and political foundation for a just and humane society—unlike any before it or since. Fidelity to these principles abolished slavery, just as they can ensure the civil society's longevity. The mastermind and his followers mostly ignore the Declaration and pick the Constitution like an old scab. As I wrote in *Liberty and Tyranny*, "The Modern Liberal believes in the supremacy of the state, thereby rejecting the principles of the Declaration and the order of the civil society, in whole or part. For the Modern Liberal, the individual's imperfection and personal pursuits impede the objective of a utopian state. In this, Modern Liberalism promotes what . . . Tocqueville described as a soft tyranny, which becomes increasingly more oppressive, potentially leading to a hard tyranny (some form of totalitarianism). As the word 'liberal' is, in its classical meaning, the opposite of authoritarian, it is more accurate . . . to characterize the Modern Liberal as a *Statist*."[27]

Utopianism is not new. It has been repackaged countless times—since Plato and before. It is as old as tyranny itself. In democracies, its practitioners legislate without end. In America, law is piled upon law in contravention and contradiction of the governing law—the Constitution. But there are no *actual* masterminds who, upon election or appointment, are magically imbued with godlike qualities. There are pretenders with power, lots of power. When they are not rebelling they are dictating, but the ultimate objective is always the same—control over the individual in order to control society. They are adamantly committed to their abstraction and their accumulation of authority to pursue it, to devastating effect. Accordingly, its exploration in this book—from Plato's *Republic* to what I term modern-day *Ameritopia*—is essential to understanding the nature and influence of this force on American society today.

CHAPTER TWO

PLATO'S *REPUBLIC* AND THE PERFECT SOCIETY

PLATO WAS NOT THE first but he was among the most prominent of the earliest philosophers to develop a utopian state model.
Plato's *Republic*[1] was written in approximately 380 BCE. Applying
his notions of a just society, Plato claimed to construct an "ideal
city" through a fictional dialogue between Socrates and others. In
fact, what he created is a totalitarian state. Although there has
been much discussion among scholars throughout the centuries
about Plato's intent in writing the *Republic*, his most prominent
critic was none other than his onetime student, Aristotle. Nonetheless, the *Republic*'s influence on subsequent philosophers and
societies is clear. It is not difficult to find the germs of Marxism,
National Socialism, Islamicism, and other forms of utopianism

in the *Republic*. Indeed, while all particulars clearly are not relevant, the *Republic*'s grand attempt to create the perfect society resonates throughout Western democracies, despite its rejection of democracy.

Plato's first proposal for the *Republic*'s Ideal City is described as a "true and healthy" model for utopian life. This city provides for only the most basic needs of its citizens—food, shelter, clothing, and shoes. It is constructed on a simple division of labor where each individual does a single job based on his most productive skills. Each individual accepts his position in the City and does what he is supposed to do for the benefit of himself and the other citizens. He does this because all of his needs are met.

There is no competition among the citizens, and since the City is perfectly just, there is no need for a government. The Ideal City does not have any luxuries—including furniture, entertainment, and meat (369–372c).

Plato acknowledges that this most basic city is not one with which many will be satisfied, because of its overly simple way of life (373a). Therefore, he constructs another Ideal City, which he describes as "feverish" and "luxurious," but which accommodates human desire (372e). In truth, what it promotes is, for most, the individual's subservience to the state—state control of private property, health care, the workforce, housing, and more. It establishes a strict class system and uses eugenics, euthanasia, arranged marriages, and the ongoing indoctrination of the masses to maintain unity in the "just society." And it is built on a foundation of falsehoods, propaganda, and censorship. The intention is to create an aristocratic ruling class of philosophers—Guardians—who will rule wisely and guide the City.[2] Of course, there is little to prevent the ruling class from abusing its power and ruling on its own behalf, as history has demonstrated time and again.

The "feverish" City will allow certain luxuries, like "sofas and tables and other furniture; also dainties and perfumes and incense and courtesans, and cakes . . . and gold and ivory and all sorts of materials [that] must be procured" (373a). The Guardians determine who gets what.

The Ideal City will then need to enlarge its borders as it will "fill and swell with a multitude of callings which are not required by any natural want. . . ." (373b) Pasture and tillage land will also be needed, which Plato argues will have to come from neighboring cities, which will also threaten expansion (373d). This will require the City to develop the capacity to make war (373d). A warrior class of Auxiliaries must, therefore, be cultivated (373e–374a). They will be trained to be aggressive and ruthless, but must also be controlled so as to keep them gentle toward the citizens of the City (375e). The Auxiliaries serve the Guardians, the latter being the only class trained in reason. The Guardians are to be a pure race of leaders, originally bred from the best citizens (415a).

Plato takes his class structure very far. He invents the "noble lie"—a contrivance taught from the earliest age that each person is born of the earth rather than from a mother. Moreover, each individual is said to be born with a particular metal—gold, silver, or bronze—intermingled in his or her body. The metal determines the person's status and relative worth in the City—the gold-souled citizens are the Guardians, the silver-souled citizens are the Auxiliaries, and the bronze-souled citizens are the Producers (although they are treated more like slaves) (415a).

The City's unity and stability, essential in the *Republic*, require that its citizens be conditioned to accept their positions and surrender their personal desires to the needs of the City. The individual's happiness is secondary to the general welfare of the City. Individuals are conditioned to suppress their personal desires in favor of acting for the common good. "The noble lie," therefore, is supposedly necessary because it promotes universal acceptance of the individual's class status. Citizens will feel more kinship with the City, eliminate political factionalism and civil strife, and promote patriotism (415d).

The City is structured to exercise absolute control, a top priority being to ensure purity within the classes. The Guardians have among their most important duties the strict regulation of the birth of children and, hence, the sexual activity of adults (415b). Only gold men may mate with gold women, and so on with the other classes. Sexual partners are chosen based on a phony lottery system, the outcome of which is arranged in advance by the Guardians. If somehow a bronze child manages to be born to a gold parent, the child is removed and sent to live among the bronze people (415c).

In the *Republic*, Plato also promotes eugenics—that is, the creation of a pure race. A "first principle" for rulers is "above all else, that there is nothing which [the rulers] should so anxiously guard, or of which they are to be such good guardians, as the purity of the race" (415b). The purity of the race is maintained through state-managed sexual activity—"the best of either sex should be united with the best as often, and the inferior with the inferior as seldom as possible. . . . Now these goings on must be kept secret which the rulers only know. . . . We shall have to invent some ingenious kind of lots which the less worthy may draw on each occasion of our bringing them together, and then they will accuse their own ill luck and not the rulers" (459d–460a).

Obviously, the nuclear family is abolished. Men, women, and children live communally (423a). Children are removed from their mothers soon after birth and raised and educated collectively. The City replaces parents and their contemporaries become their brothers and sisters (414d). The purpose is to create a single extended family—the City itself. In this way, the individual will presumably become loyal to and reliant on the City, thereby eliminating competitiveness between the City and family.

Plato argues that private property has the potential of corrupting the Guardians, who are to act solely in the City's best interests. Therefore, they are to own no property. Plato writes: "Then now let us consider what will be their way of life, if they are to realize our idea of them. In the first place, none of them should have any property of his beyond what is absolutely necessary; neither should they have a private house or store closed against anyone who has a mind to enter; their provisions should be only such as are required by trained warriors, who are men of temperance and courage; they should agree to receive from the citizens a fixed rate of pay, enough to meet the expenses of the year and no more; and they will go to mess and live together like soldiers in camp. . . ." (416d–e)

The purpose of "both the community of property and the community of families . . . tend[s] to make them more truly Guardians; they will not tear the City in pieces by differing about 'mine' and 'not mine'; each man dragging any acquisition which he has made into a separate house of his own, where he has a separate wife and children and private pains and pleasures; but all will be affected as far as may be by the same wife and children and private pleasures and pains because they are all of one opinion about what is near and dear to them, and therefore they all tend toward a common end. . . . And as they have nothing but their persons which they can call their own, suits and complaint will have no existence among them; they will be delivered from all those quarrels of which money or children or relations are the occasion" (464d–e).

Indoctrination is also crucial to controlling the citizenry. The City consists of a comprehensive "education" system." In addition to the "noble lie," censorship is widely practiced. For example, myths and music are suppressed to avoid any stories where authority is challenged or the Guardians are presented as anything other than good (379c). The style of music is regulated. Only certain modes and rhythms are approved, for "rhythm and harmony most of all insinuate themselves into the inner most part of the soul and most vigorously lay hold of it" (401d). Freedom of expression is banned for the Ideal City's health is more important than self-expression.

Having eliminated family ties, independent thought, and individual dignity, Plato turns to the City's standards for medical ethics. Only those who are otherwise healthy, but suffer either an injury or a seasonal malady, are entitled to medical care. The chronically ill are not beneficial to the City and will not be treated. "Medicine should not treat bodies diseased through and through" or those with "a naturally sickly body" (407d). The old and infirm are also denied treatment. "No one has the leisure to be sick throughout life" and should not benefit from "the invention of lingering death" (406b–c). Illnesses resulting from idleness or inactivity are not to be treated. Plato also proposes state-imposed euthanasia for appropriate cases as determined by the Guardians.

With the City's construction completed, Plato explains his program for educating the Guardians and developing from their ranks the wisest and most just "philosopher" kings.

Underlying Plato's ruling philosophers and the Ideal City is the notion of "Forms" and "the Good." The Theory of the Forms guides Plato's search for the Good. Forms are by their nature independent from the sensible and physical world and are a sort of ultimate, perfect example of a thing or being.[3] The idea of "the Good" is similar to the biblical concept of God or ultimate truth. It is the cause of knowledge and truth, but is beyond them both (508e). The Good is not being but is beyond being. In Plato's *Republic*, the Good governs all aspects of life. In his view, however, contemplating the Good and understanding the Good are far beyond the capabilities of the vast majority of people. Consequently, the City must be ruled by philosophers for they are the only people who are able to discern the Good. Only the philosopher can make judgments about what constitutes a "good person," a "good life," or a "good death." Good is synonymous with quality and is measured by an individual's contribution to the City. "Philosophers because of their love of the Forms, become lovers of proper order in the sensible world as well. They wish to imitate the harmony of the Forms, and so in their relations with others they are loathe to do anything that violates the proper order among people."[4]

Identifying and training philosophers from the Guardian class is a decades-long process. For the first twenty years of life, all ruling-class children are educated in "gymnastics" (training the body) and "music" (training the mind in art and literature). At age twenty, the most accomplished students are chosen for "higher honor"—additional educational training in mathematics (plane geometry, solid geometry, harmonics, theoretical astronomy, and the introduction into the study of philosophy). (526c, 528b, 529, and 537c)

After ten years of intense training, the finest of these thirty-year-old students are selected for additional honor, training, and position. Those not selected are sent to careers in the military and government. Plato warns that the rulers must be especially careful to weed out entirely artistic students who are "filled with lawlessness" and are a great threat to the City (537e).

This select group is the most elite of all and is given five years to undertake the great honor of studying philosophy (539c). Then, for fifteen years, they become involved in the practical study of government, immersing themselves in the ways of the world. "[A]t the end of the time they must be sent down again into the den and compelled to hold any military or other office which young men are qualified to hold: in this way they will get their experience of life, and there will be an opportunity of trying whether, when they are drawn all manner of ways by temptation, they will stand firm or flinch" (540a). At the age of fifty, those who have distinguished themselves in every "action of their lives, and in every branch of knowledge" are ready to devote their lives to philosophy for the purpose of determining how best to rule the City (540a). From this group is chosen the leader, who rules not because he desires power, but because he knows it is his duty to be a wise and just ruler for the public good (540b). The Ideal City is complete.

Yet, Plato predicts that despite his just and wise City, it would be nearly impossible to create and, if created, would be impossible to maintain, given man's imperfections.

First, Plato states that the City would only be possible when the true philosopher-kings are born in a State "despising the honors of this present world" (540e). This could only happen when the entire City is raised in Plato's education and class system. Plato declares that no one over the age of ten can be among the City's first citizens (541a). Of course, children would have to be removed from their families with the parents' consent or their parents would have to be eliminated to meet this requirement. Plato believes neither of these options is likely to occur.

Second, Plato acknowledges the impossibility of regulating sexual reproduction (546a). "All the wisdom and education of your rulers will not attain; the laws which regulate them will not be discovered by an intelligence which is alloyed with sense, but will escape them, and they will bring children into the world when they ought not" (546b). In short, human passion cannot be regulated by any mathematical formula, class structure, or state directive.

The resulting uncontrolled intermingling of gold, silver, and bronze citizens leads to the dilution of the pure race and the downward spiral from the wise and just City to a brutal tyranny. The first phase is a "timocracy," which is rule by a class of honorable but conflicted rulers (545d). The rulers revere honor in their official public life but are dissatisfied with the modest life they and their families lead. Over time, their commitment to honor is overtaken by their (and their spouses') passion for wealth (549b). The honorable rulers' children see this conflict and become obsessed with the acquisition of money, at first to please their parents, but in the end to satisfy their own obsession (549d). They become the next set of rulers, who form an oligarchy—that is, rule by a wealthy few. They encourage the citizenry to borrow money from the rulers and, in turn, drive the citizens into poverty because they cannot repay their debts to the oligarchs (555c). The oligarchs refuse to spend money on such basic needs as education or a military (551e, 552e). In the end, the impoverished and resentful citizenry rise up and easily overthrow the oligarchy. In its place they install a democracy (557a).

Plato has harsh criticism for the democracy and in particular many of the democracy's citizens. He admits, however, that the democracy is the fairest and freest of the systems he describes (557c). But he argues that freedom and fairness without education and discipline is a recipe for disaster. The majority of citizens become undisciplined and easily seduced by unnecessary desires (558d). The oligarchs' deprivation and impoverishment of the citizenry causes the people to engage in vices and excess (561c–d). Tradition and authority are rejected for obsession with freedom (562e–563a).

Plato illustrates his concerns with familiar examples: parents treat their children as contemporaries and the children, in turn, disrespect and disobey their parents as a sign of their freedom (562e); teachers flatter their students out of fear and the students disrespect their teachers (563a); and the citizens "chafe at the least touch of authority . . . and cease to care even for the laws, written or unwritten; they will have no one over them" (563e).

Plato warns that the excesses that dominate the democracy will lead the undisciplined majority to become drunk with freedom (502d). As a result, the rulers must constantly strive to please the citizens (565a).

Eventually a great champion appears whom the people "set over them and nurse into greatness" (565c). He is seen as the citizens' protector (565c–d). He is the ultimate populist, but is in fact a demagogue—the great panderer of the people (566e). Plato warns that the protector will become obsessed with power, the consolidation of power, and the preservation of power. He loses sight of the community's well-being and can only see himself. Finally, he seizes absolute power as a political tyrant and the City becomes the most miserable of cities (576d).[5]

Plato, born of an aristocratic family, concludes: "Just as the philosopher is the best and happiest of men, so the aristocratic State is the best and happiest of States; and just as the tyrannical despot, the slave of ambition and passion, is the worst and most unhappy of men, so is the State ruled by the tyrant the worst and most unhappy of States."[6] For Plato, the tyrant and the philosopher have much in common. Both have a passionate love—the philosopher for wisdom; the tyrant for political power (573b).

The Ideal City is neither ideal nor a republic. Plato built and rebuilt his utopian society in the *Republic* and then abandoned it. Why? To his great credit, he accepted its impossibility, but it is unclear whether he believed its various manifestations were undesirable. He appears resigned to mankind's inability to conform to his models. Plato insists the City cannot be built upon experience. He requires a clean slate. However, there is no way to effectively clear the mind of the supposed clutter of history and limit knowledge to that which has yet to come.

In the *Republic*, Plato is openly hostile to individualism, which he believes destructive of the collective good of the Ideal City. Although Plato is clearly exploring a wide range of human characteristics, including knowledge, education, family relations, etc., he does so not to embrace human nature, but to shape and order it. In so many ways, he drains the individual's lifeblood of free will and self-interest.

Yet, as Karl Popper, a critic of Plato and the *Republic*, wrote, "This individualism, united with altruism, has become the basis of western civilization. It is the central doctrine of Christianity ('love your neighbor,' say the Scriptures, not 'love your tribe'); and it is the core of all ethical doctrines which have grown from our civilization and stimulated it. . . . There is no other thought which has been so powerful in the moral development of man. Plato was right when he saw in this doctrine the enemy of his caste state; and he hated it more than any other of the 'subversive' doctrines of his time."[7]

Plato's caste system assigns roles and duties to people as if they are not people at all, based on his own preconceptions and prejudices. In this way, the individual loses his identity and can be directed toward the City's best interests. Ultimately, therefore, it is the rulers for which the City exists. These are Plato's masterminds. Only they are smart enough and expert enough, by birth and training, to properly manage the City. As Plato wrote, "Unless either philosophers become kings in our states or those whom we now call our kings and rulers take to the pursuit of philosophy seriously and adequately, and there is a conjunction of these two things, political power and philosophic intelligence, while the motley horde of the natures who at present pursue either apart

from the other are compulsorily excluded, there can be no cessa-
tion of troubles . . . for our states, nor, I fancy, for the human race
either" (473c–d). In the *Republic*, it is as if Plato built a society
over which he and the students of his Academy would rule—an
elitism of philosopher-kings hatched of the same sort of arrogance
too often found in the modern academy. Yet the overtones of
egalitarianism persist, for within the three classes of the *Republic*,
the individuals are mostly indistinguishable. They live as political,
social, and economic equals without autonomy or even their own
identities.

It is possible the *Republic* reflects Plato's hostility toward the
fragile, off-and-on-again Athenian democracy that took the life
of Socrates—Plato's mentor and teacher—and represents Plato's
search for a "just" alternative. Socrates was considered a threat
to the teetering Athenian government for his unrelenting and
provocative questioning of its personages, institutions, and morality. But the intellectual methodology for which Socrates is
known is denied most inhabitants of Plato's City. The "Socratic
method" of inquiry, in which the common beliefs of the day are
challenged through a dialectic process of questions and answers,
is intended to sort out the weaknesses, strengthens, objections,
alternatives, or support for those beliefs. But in the City, the individual is indentured to the state. Justice is synonymous with the
well-being of the City. The classes exist to work as a harmonious
collective to ensure order. Dissent, independence, and change are
considered destructive. Ironically, it is unlikely Socrates would
have survived long in Plato's City, given its totalitarian com-
plexion.

Popper observed that "Plato . . . became, unconsciously, the pioneer of the many propagandists who, often in good faith, developed the technique of appealing to the moral, humanitarian sentiments, for anti-humanitarian, immoral purposes. . . . He transfigured his hatred of individual initiative, and his wish to arrest all change, into a love of justice and temperance, of a heavenly state in which everybody is satisfied and happy and in which the crudity of money-grabbing is replaced by laws of generosity and friendship. . . . It is the expression of, and an ardent appeal to, the sentiments of those who suffer from the strain of civilization. (It is part of the strain that we are becoming more and more painfully aware of the gross imperfections in our life, of personal as well as institutional imperfection; of avoidable suffering, of waste and of unnecessary ugliness; and at the same time the fact that it is not impossible for us to do something about all this, but that such improvements would be just as hard to achieve as they are important. This awareness increases the strain of personal responsibility, of carrying the cross of being human.)"[8]

One profound lesson Plato teaches, albeit not by design, is that Plato himself, considered by many the greatest of all philosophers, could not construct the perfect society. He sought to avoid the disintegration of society and the onset of tyranny, but his solution was a totalitarian City destructive of human nature. Regrettably, Plato provided a philosophical and intellectual brew for a utopian society that would influence tyrannies for centuries to come.[9]

CHAPTER THREE

THOMAS MORE'S *UTOPIA* AND RADICAL EGALITARIANISM

THE WORD *UTOPIA* WAS coined by Sir Thomas More, a noted British barrister, lord chancellor under King Henry VIII, and since recognized as a saint in the Catholic Church. More created utopia as the centerpiece of his novel by the same name in 1516.[1] The book is an extended, Socratic-style conversation between More, a friend of his named Peter Giles of Antwerp (where the story takes place), Cardinal Morton of Antwerp, and a fictional world traveler named Raphael Hythloday.

The discussion includes a variety of topics relating to how a monarch should govern and the kinds of counsel that should be offered to a prince or a king by his advisers. "For whereas your Plato judgeth that weal publics shall by this means attain perfect

felicity," More explained in his extended dialogue, "either if philosophers be kings, or else if kings give themselves to the study of
philosophy . . ." (43)

During the lengthy conversations that comprise Book One,
Hythloday makes several references to an island nation he has
visited in the New World (in the story, Hythloday was part of
the real-life explorer Amerigo Vespucci's expedition to the New
World [17]. It is during this journey that Hythloday encounters
the island nation of Utopia). In order to observe and understand
the nation, its people, and its mores, Hythloday decided to live
among the island natives for five years.

In Book Two, More describes Utopia in all its intricate detail.
It was named after King Utopus, the first great king who united
the people living on what was then a peninsula. When Utopus
saw that people from neighboring towns and cities might present
a cultural threat to the people of Utopia, he ordered that a fifteen-
mile-wide trench be dug across the top of the peninsula, creating
the island of Utopia and separating it from the mainland, thereby
making it easier for the utopians to maintain their societal and
cultural purity. ". . . King Utopus, whose name as conqueror the
island beareth . . . —which also brought the rude and wild people
to that excellent perfection in all good fashions, humanity, and
civil gentleness, wherein they now go beyond all the people of
the world—even at his first arriving and entering upon the land,
forthwith obtaining the victory, caused fifteen miles space of up-
landish ground, where the sea had no passage, to be cut and digged
up, and so brought the sea round the land" (62).

Hythloday's underlying contention throughout the narrative
is that a society in which every need is answered and every want

is either met or made results in near-perfect existence. "But now will I declare how the citizens use themselves one towards another; what familiar occupying and entertainment there is among the people; and what fashion they use in the distribution of every thing" (76). Utopia is planned down to the most minor detail. There are fifty-four cities on the island, each virtually identical in size, structure, and organization. "There is in the island fifty-four large and fair cities, or shire towns. . . . They be all set and situate alike, and in all fashioned alike, as far forth as the place or plot suffereth" (63). The cities are approximately twenty-four miles apart. This means that no city is farther than a day's journey by foot from any other municipality (63).

Each city has a maximum of 6,000 individuals within its borders, organized into families (63, 76). If, in any city, the number of citizens grows beyond 6,000, the excess inhabitants are forcibly relocated to other cities with fewer than the maximum number, or moved into the countryside to form a new town. "This measure or number is easily observed and kept by putting them that in fuller families be above the number into families of smaller increase. But if chance be that in the whole city the store increase above the just number, therewith they fill up the lack of other cities. But if so be that the multitude throughout the whole island pass and exceed the due number, then they choose out of every city certain citizens and build up a town under their own laws in the next land where the inhabitants have much waste and unoccupied ground, receiving also of the same country people to them, if they will join and dwell with them . . ." (77).

Outside of each city are identical farms with no fewer than forty people on each farm, in addition to two bondmen, or slaves.

Each farm is ruled by the oldest man and woman in the family (63). Every thirty farms is ruled by a head bailiff, called a Phylarch in the Utopian language, who is elected annually by the families (68). At harvest time each year, the Phylarchs tell the magistrates within the city how many additional people will be necessary to harvest the crops; the magistrates order the requested number of citizens within the city to assist with the harvest. "When their harvest day draweth near and is at hand, then the phylarchs, which be the head officers and bailiffs of husbandry, send word to the magistrates of the city what number of harvest men is needful to be sent to them out of the city. The which company of harvest men, being ready at the day appointed, almost in one fair day dispatcheth all the harvest work" (65). The same sort of draft of citizens is also initiated by the magistrates to repair the island's roads, if need be (76).

Because every citizen of Utopia is expected to be intimately familiar with farming and agriculture, every two years twenty people from each farm are ordered to live in the neighboring city. Every home in every city is required to have a vegetable garden (67). At the end of the two-year period, the city and farm dwellers switch places (64).

Each family has between ten and sixteen children (77). Women may not marry before the age of eighteen, men before the age of twenty-two (108). Family members in excess of that limit are required to join another family. Each family is trained in a specific trade or vocation, with the children expected to carry on the specialty from generation to generation. Individuals are allowed to pursue other interests, but they must join another family that specializes in the desired vocation—that is, if you want to change vocations, you must also change families. "But if a man's mind stand to any other, he is by adoption put into a family of that occupation which he doth most fantasy, whom not only his father but also the magistrates do diligently look to, that he be put to a discreet and an honest householder" (70, 71).

Recall that each year, every thirty families choose the Phylarch. Every ten Phylarchs elect a chief Phylarch known as a Tranibore. There are two hundred Phylarchs in each city. They elect the Prince. The Prince rules for life but cannot pass on his post to his offspring. The Phylarchs elect a new prince upon the death of the old one. The Tranibores serve as an advisory and governing council with the Prince. They meet every third day. Their meetings are conducted in secret and members are prohibited from discussing council business in public under penalty of death—with one exception: the most serious issues are taken by the Tranibores to the Phylarchs, who in turn bring the matter to their respective families. The families' decisions are then brought back to the council of Tranibores for final action. An island-wide council composed of three of the wisest men from each of the cities assembles annually in the capital city of Amaurote. By law, on Utopia the governing council must debate three days on every issue brought before it. Moreover, no dispute or issue may be voted on by the council the same day in which it is raised for debate (63, 68, 69). Consequently, in Utopia, More creates the outline of a representative governmental structure. However, it is largely irrelevant, given the established dictates affecting minute details of daily life.

* * *

Citizens may not travel either within or beyond their city's limits without a passport issued by the Prince. If a person is caught traveling without a passport, they can be punished severely (82). Each house in Utopia's fifty-four cities is identical to every other house and no one owns the home or farm on which they live. There is, in fact, no such thing as private property of any kind on Utopia (67).

Utopia's economic egalitarianism requires everyone to turn over everything they produce to central storehouses, from where they, in turn, get whatever they require to live. "Thither the works of every family be brought into houses, and every kind of thing is laid up several in barns or storehouses. From hence the father of every family or every householder fetcheth whatsoever he and his have need of then carrieth it away with him without money, without exchange, without gage, pawn, or pledge. For why should any thing be called unto him, seeing there is abundance of all things and that it is not to be feared lest any man will ask more than he needeth? For why should it be thought that that man would ask more than enough, which is sure never to lack?" (78) There are no poor people. "This fashion and trade of life being used among the people, it cannot be chosen but they must of necessity have store and plenty of all things. And seeing they be all thereof partners equally, therefore, can no man there be poor or needy" (84). Indeed, in Utopia, money is considered the source of much evil. For that reason no one is paid for their labor in currency, which is banned from the island. Gold, silver, and other precious metals have no value. Instead, they are used in chamber pots and other items used for the less than savory personal tasks in daily life (86). "[A]ll the desire of money with the use thereof is utterly secluded and banished, how great a heap of cares is cut away!

How great an occasion of wickedness and mischief is plucked up by the roots! For who knoweth not that fraud, theft, ravin, brawling, quarreling, babbling, strife, chiding, contention, murder, treason, poisoning, which by daily punishments are rather revenged than refrained, do die when money dieth? And also that fear, grief, care, labors, and watchings do perish even the very same moment that money perisheth? Yea, poverty itself, which only seemed to lack money, if money were gone, it also would decrease and vanish away" (144).

As noted earlier, daily life in Utopia is strictly regimented. The chief duty of the Phylarchs is to ensure that the people follow the schedules established for them each day and that no one is idle (71). There is only a six-hour workday, three hours in the morning and three hours in the afternoon, after a mandatory two-hour rest following lunch. Bedtime for everyone is 8 P.M. All must sleep for eight hours (71). In their off hours, outside of work and sleep, Utopians are expected to pursue whatever hobbies or avocations interest them but which will also contribute to the greater good of the island nation. Meals are taken communally at appointed times in a great hall in each neighborhood. There are also strict requirements about where the men, women, and children sit. It is legal for an individual to eat the occasional fruit or vegetable from the gardens that are grown in the backyards of every home (80).

People all wear identical clothing and it is against the law to affect adornments of any kind. "For their garments, which throughout all the island be of one fashion . . . and this one continueth for evermore unchanged, seemly and comely to the eye, no let to the moving and wielding of the body, also fit both for winter and summer—as for these garments (I say) every family maketh their

own" (70). The only exceptions are at festivals, where everyone
but the priests wear white (139).

Every religion on the island must recognize a single, supreme,
ubiquitous god. Priests within the leading religion on the island
are among the most highly esteemed people in the utopian society
(134). The churches, which are limited in number but very large
and elegant, are open to all worshippers. "The common sacrifices
be so ordered that they be in no derogation nor prejudice to any of
the private sacrifices or religions. Therefore, no image of any god is
seen in the church, to see to the intent it may be free for every man
to conceive God by their religion after what likeness and simili-
tude they will. They call upon no peculiar name of God, but only
Mythra, in the which word they all agree together in one nature of
the devine majesty whatsoever it be" (137, 138).

Since there is no private property on the island, and no currency for domestic use, every health-care service is free. Four hospitals are strategically located outside each city. They are great
structures, lavishly appointed and extremely well equipped. "For in
the circuit of the city . . . they have four hospitals, so big, so wide,
so ample, and so large, that they may seem four little towns. . . .
These hospitals be so well appointed, and with all things necessary
to health so furnished . . . there is no sick person in all the city
that had not rather lie there than at home in his own house" (79).
However, death is not feared but celebrated among Utopians.
People who die have an opportunity to meet their maker (131).
Therefore, individuals who suffer from incurable diseases or fatal
conditions, and who are no longer of use to the society in general,
are encouraged to commit suicide to ease their pain and alleviate the burden they represent to island civilization. "They that be

thus persuaded finish their lives willingly, either with hunger, or else die in their sleep without any feeling of death" (107).

Although private property, currency, and precious metals have no value in the utopian world, the country does maintain the monies that are paid by cities and nations with which Utopia trades. These funds are kept to pay for the use of mercenaries to fight the odd war with other cities and nations that may occasionally arise. Also, Utopia does not engage in the contemporaneous practices of appropriating the wealth or enslaving the civilian populations of the nations it conquers. Only the combatants who actually fought in battle against Utopia's forces are taken into slavery.

Nearly five hundred years after *Utopia* was first published, scholars still debate whether it was intended to be, in whole or part, a serious statement of political theory, More's preferred ideal society, or a fiction supposedly built on humanism. Whatever his intended approach, More obviously meant for his work to have meaning, which it has for centuries.

The crux of More's critique, delivered through Hythloday, seems clear—his revulsion with the injustices and inequities of society at the time: "Here now would I see if any man dare be so bold as to compare with this equity the justice of other nations, among whom I forsake God if I can find any sign or token of equity and justice. For what justice is this, that a rich goldsmith, or an usurer, or, to be short, any of them which either do nothing at all, or else that which they do is such that it is not very necessary to the commonwealth, should have a pleasant and a wealthy living either by idleness or by unnecessary business, when in the meantime poor laborers, carters, ironsmiths, carpenters, and plowmen, by so great and continual toil as drawing and bearing beasts be scant able to sustain, and again so unnecessary toil that without it no common-wealth were able to continue and endure one year, should yet get so hard and poor a living, and live so wretched and miserable a life, that the state and condition of the laboring beasts may seem much better and wealthier? For they be not put to so continual labor, nor their living is not much worse, yea, to them much pleasanter, taking no thought in the mean season for the time to come. But these silly poor wretches be presently tormented with barren and unfruitful labor, and the remembrance of their poor, indigent, and beggarly old age killeth them up. For their daily wages is so little that it will not suffice for the same day, much less it yieldeth any overplus that may faily be laid up for the relief of old age" (142).

Moreover, for More, the individual's pride is his greatest mal-ady and destructive of the sameness and oneness of purpose so cru-cial to a just society. "And I doubt not that either the respect of every man's private commodity or else the authority of our savior Christ . . . would have brought all the world long ago into the law of this weal public, if it were not that one only beast, the princess and mother of all mischief, Pride, doth withstand and let it. She measureth not wealth and prosperity by her own commodities, but by the misery and incommodities of others; she would not by her good will be made a goddess, if there were no wretches left over whom she might, like a scornful lady, rule and triumph, over whose miseries her felicities might shine, whose poverty she might vex, torment, and increase by gorgeously setting forth her riches. This hell-hound creepth into men's hearts and plucketh them back from entering the right path of life and is so deeply rooted in men's breasts that she cannot be plucked out" (144, 145).

• • •

More's response is to fabricate an egalitarian society that claims to provide for all wants and needs on an equal basis by expunging humanness from the human being and suppressing individual pride—that is, free will and personal fulfillment—for the good of society. In *Utopia*, the individual is not trusted to care for himself. His highest value is that of an insipid worker compliantly obeying orders. His personality must be reengineered. His own desires and happiness, therefore, are made indistinguishable from those of every other individual. More controls the individual and his environment, which extends to the most basic aspects of life.

Despite the establishment of representative councils, the power of the state is nearly absolute, for the problem, as usual, is not the utopian fantasy, which is self-evidently prophetic, but the flawed individual who is unable, on his own, to live up to it. As a result, people are forced to work on farms, move to different homes, and join other families. They must wear the same type of clothing, live in the same style homes, and reside in similarly designed towns. They eat, sleep, and dress as told. The individual is constantly prodded, yanked, and pushed to do that which he may not wish to do. He is even encouraged to self-euthanize when his illness or weakness interferes with his ability to contribute to society. But for those few who become, for example, Phylarchs and Tranibores, all citizens must be involved in farming and other forms of manual labor. Thus, even more thoroughly than the *Republic*, More's *Utopia* demands conformity, uniformity, and communal living for nearly all of its inhabitants. Apart from its religious component, it is similar in kind to, and a forerunner to, the "utopian socialism" in *The Communist Manifesto* and its emphasis on radical egalitarianism.

Of course, *Utopia* is no paradise. It substitutes one evil for another. Like the *Republic*, *Utopia* misapprehends man's nature. Rather than nurture it, *Utopia* suppresses it. Among other things, More does not amply tackle the necessity of his ideal society to establish a far-reaching administrative and enforcement apparatus to oversee his society's intricate rules. While he metes out punishment for certain indiscretions and offenses, the coercion and repression required to impose order must be more elaborate and brutal than More acknowledges. For example, surely stubborn resistance by some if not most families to the forced separation of its members, or the relocation of citizens from cities to farms to work the fields whether they want to or not, would require police-state tactics to effectuate. It is reminiscent of Mao Zedong's Great Leap Forward, which was instituted more than 440 years later, resulting in the death of millions of Chinese. Furthermore, while *Utopia* provides a form of representative government, More does not explain how such a government can exist within the framework of a thoroughly controlled cultural and economic climate, the purpose of which is to denude the citizen of his individuality (pride); or whether it can exist as the carefully planned society More intended should the families vote for representatives to undo the supposed ideal parts of his society.

Utopia's peninsula is also turned into an island for the purpose of isolating its citizens from the rest of the world, with some exceptions. Mobility within and outside the island is monitored and strictly regulated by the Prince himself. By severely limiting external influences and interactions of most kinds, More's paradise would undoubtedly stagnate and regress—economically, intellectually, scientifically, technologically, culturally, etc.—for the flow of information and access to knowledge that contributes to the vitality, growth, and energy of a society are largely proscribed, much like many of the communist regimes of the twentieth and twenty-first centuries.

Although More was an enormously courageous man of deep faith, executed by King Henry VIII for his principled refusal to disparage the Roman Catholic Church, and although his invention, *Utopia,* was, I believe, intended as a humane response to the contemporary society that undoubtedly troubled him, More was no more successful than Plato. *Utopia* is a tyrannical society, destructive of individual sovereignty and free will, with many of the attributes of a communist state.

CHAPTER FOUR

THOMAS HOBBES'S *LEVIATHAN* AND THE ALL-POWERFUL STATE

THOMAS HOBBES WAS A partisan of the English royalty who was appalled by the series of civil wars between the English Royalists and Parliamentarians, religious turmoil, and general anarchy that led to the execution of Charles I. He fled to France where, in 1651, he wrote *Leviathan*,[1] which was influenced by what he had observed and experienced.

Hobbes argued that as men live in a constant state of fear, anxiety, and conflict, they could not be trusted to govern themselves. As such, a "Sovereign" must be given absolute power over men ("Subjects") to protect them against themselves and outside invaders (a Sovereign can either be a single person such as a Monarch, or an assembly of men). The Sovereign was an all-powerful

Leviathan—a totalitarian state with a vast bureaucracy controlling the lives of its Subjects.

Submission to the Leviathan (or Commonwealth) meant transferring one's rights to the Sovereign. That way, Hobbes believed men could live in peace, stability, and contentment. The rights transferred included, among others, control of the judicial system (what is right or wrong), control of Subjects' free will (what Subjects could or could not do), control of Subjects' possessions (what goods the Subject could enjoy), distribution of materials such as land, and control over foreign trade. Hobbes described this relationship as a social contract or compact.

Hobbes argued that men are equal in the sense that all individuals strive for survival. Even a strong man can be compromised by a confederation of physically or mentally weaker men. "Nature hath made men so equal in the faculties of body and mind as that, though there be found one man sometimes manifestly stronger in body or of quicker mind than another, yet when all is reckoned together the differences between man and man is not so considerable as that one man can thereupon claim to himself any benefit to which another may not pretend as well as he" (74). The problem is when "any two men [of equal hopes] desire the same thing, which nevertheless they cannot both enjoy, they become enemies; and in the way to their end, which is principally their own conservation, and sometimes their delectation only, endeavour to destroy or subdue one another" (75). Anarchy ensues as men cannot secure themselves from the collective force of other men and men can also seek to exercise power over other men. Thus, men have no pleasure but, instead, grief (75). "So that in the nature of man we find three principal causes of quarrel: first, competition; secondly, diffidence; thirdly, glory. The first maketh men invade for gain; the second, for safety; and the third, for reputation" (76).

In this state of war, where the individual seeks his own preservation, and where "every man [is] against every man, this also is consequent: that nothing can be unjust. The notions of right and wrong, justice and injustice, have there no place. Where there is no common power, there is no law; where there is no law, no injustice. Force and fraud are in war the two cardinal virtues. Justice and injustice are none of the faculties neither of body, nor mind. . . . They are qualities that relate to men in society, not in solitude" (78).

Hobbes concluded that the state of man in the state of nature is a state of war. "[T]he condition of man . . . is a condition of war of everyone against everyone. . . ." (80) As such, man believes he has a right to everything, even to another man's body. As long as man believes it is his natural right to everything there can be no security to any other man to live his full life (80).

Hobbes famously declared, "Whatsoever therefore is consequent to a time of war, where every man is enemy to every man, the same is consequent to the time wherein men live without other security than what their own invention shall furnish them withal. In such condition there is no place for industry, because the fruit thereof is uncertain, and consequently, no culture of the earth, no navigation, nor use of the commodities that may be imported by sea, no commodious building, no instruments of moving and removing such things as require much force, no knowledge of the face of the earth, no account of time, no arts, no letters, no society, and which is worst of all, continual fear and danger of violent death, and the life of man, solitary, poor, nasty, brutish, and short" (76).

Yet there are also passions that incline men to peace, especially self-preservation. "The passions that incline men to peace are fear of death, desire of such things as are necessary to commodious living, and a hope by their industry to obtain them. And reason suggesteth convenient articles of peace, upon which men may be drawn to agreement." Hobbes argued there is "a precept, or general rule, of reason *that every man ought to endeavour peace, as far as he has hope of obtaining it, and when he cannot obtain it, that he may seek and use all helps and advantages of war*" (78*).

Hobbes described two Natural Laws of Contract—the transferring of rights to another in exchange for rights from another. First, man seeks peace and follows it, but when necessary defends himself. Second, man has to be willing to give up his right to all things and be content with as much liberty for himself as he would give other men (80). "To lay down a man's right to anything is to divest himself of the liberty of hindering another of the benefit of his own right to the same." "Right is laid aside either by simply renouncing it or by transferring it to another." Once a man abandons or transfers his rights he is not in the position to hinder the person who has obtained the rights from using them as they desire or see fit (81). Transferring rights can either be express or inferred (82). "Signs by inference are sometimes the consequence of words, sometimes the consequence of silence; sometimes the consequence of action; and generally a sign by inference of any contract [transfer] is whatso-

---

*NOTE: Many of the writers quoted in this book made frequent use of italic type. In the interest of accuracy, all italics appear as they did in the original documents and translations.

ever sufficiently argues the will of the contractor" (83). "[W]hen a covenant is made, then to break it is *unjust*; and the definition of INJUSTICE is no other than *the not performance of covenant*. And whatsoever is not unjust, is *just*" (89).

However, man requires a "power" to keep him in "awe" and make him fearful of punishment in order to restrain his tendencies. If no such power exists or if the power is not strong enough, men will revert to using violence and war. "[C]ovenants without the sword are but words, and of no strength to secure a man at all. Therefore . . . if there be no power erected, or not great enough for our security, every man will, and may lawfully rely on his own strength and art, for caution against other men" (106).

To create a common power to defend men from others who want to harm them, and to provide security so they can live in peace and "contently," requires that they "confer all their power and strength upon one man, or upon one assembly of men, that may reduce all their wills, by plurality of voices, unto one will . . . to appoint one man or an assembly of men to bear their person . . . and therein to submit their wills, every one to his will, and their judgments, to his judgments" (109).

"[E]very man should say to every man *I authorize and give up my right of governing myself to this man, or to this assembly of men, on this condition, that thou give up thy right to him, and authorize all his actions in a like manner.*" The uniting of all under and into one is called a "Commonwealth" or the "great Leviathan"—that is, "that *Mortal God* to which we owe, under the *Immortal God*, our peace and defence." "And in him consisteth the essence of the commonwealth, which (to define it) is *one person, of whose acts a great multitude, by mutual covenants one with another, have made themselves every*

one the author, to the end he may use the strength and means of them
all, as he shall think expedient, for their peace and common defence"
(109). The person (or persons/assembly) who is the recipient of
this transferred power is called the Sovereign. All others are his
subjects.

Sovereign power is obtained in two ways: either by Institution
(where men agree voluntarily to submit to some man or assembly
of men) or by Natural Force (through being more powerful than
another or by using war to subdue enemies). (109, 110)

The Rights of Sovereigns by Institution are nearly absolute:

RULE I: Subjects cannot change the form of government.
Subjects cannot "cast off" monarchy (the Sovereign), including making a new transfer of their rights to another
without the monarch's permission. (110)

RULE II: Sovereign Power cannot be forfeited. Once the
Subjects transfer their rights to the Sovereign they are his.
If a Subject attempts to depose or kill the Sovereign any
punishment to the Subject is a result of his own actions.
Since the Sovereign by transfer is given the rights of the
Subject, no Subject can be freed from his subjection. (111)

RULE III: Since the majority has declared a sovereign, the
minority must consent to the Sovereign's actions. Whether
he be with the majority or not, the Subject must either

"submit to their decrees or be left in the condition of war he was before." (112)

RULE IV: The Sovereign's actions cannot be "justly accused by the Subject." The Sovereign acts under the authority of Subjects who have transferred their rights to it, who is to act justly and properly. However, if the subjects complain of injury from the actions of the Sovereign they have no one to blame but themselves. "They that have Sovereign power may commit iniquity, but not injustice, or injury in the proper signification." (112, 113)

RULE V: Whatever the Sovereign does is "unpunishable" by the Subject, as every Subject is responsible for the actions of the Sovereign, and so the actions of the Sovereign are as if the Subject committed them himself. (113)

RULE VI: The Sovereign is judge for what is necessary for the "Peace and Defence" of his subjects. He is the sole judge of the means of peace and defense. He determines what is necessary to preserve peace and security, and prevent discord at home and hostility abroad, and if lost to recover peace and security. The Sovereign is the sole judge as to "what opinions and doctrines are averse" or beneficial to the Commonwealth, who can be trusted to speak to the people, and who reviews all doctrines before they are published. (113)

RULE VII: "[T]he sovereignty [has] the whole power of prescribing the rules whereby every man may know what goods he may enjoy, and what actions he may do, without being molested by any of his fellow subjects; and this is it men call property. . . . These rules of propriety . . . and of *good, evil, lawful,* and *unlawful* in the actions of subjects are the civil laws. . . ." (114)

RULE VIII: The Sovereign controls the judicial system— hearing and deciding all controversies concerning either civil or natural law. Ceding this power to the Sovereign would prevent man from settling disputes himself, thereby eliminating a condition that leads to war. (114)

RULE IX: The Sovereign is the Commander-In-Chief who decides when to wage war and against whom, the size of the army and what weapons they will have, and the ability to tax Subjects for the cost thereof. (114)

RULE X: The Sovereign chooses as he sees fit all counselors, ministers, magistrates, and officers, in both peace and war. (114, 115)

RULE XI: The Sovereign can bestow riches, honors, and punishment (corporal or pecuniary) according to the law he has made or makes. (115)

The Sovereign's Rights (or Rules) I through XI are indivisible and inseparable since they go to the heart of the purpose of the Sovereign and Commonwealth—to protect the Subjects (115, 116). The Sovereign's power must be absolute. "So that it appeareth plainly, to my understanding, both from reason and Scripture, that the sovereign power (whether placed in one man, as in monarchy, or in one assembly of men, as in popular and aristocratical commonwealths) is as great as possibly men can be imagined to make it. And though of so unlimited a power men may fancy many evil consequences, yet the consequences of the want of it, which is perpetual war of every man against his neighbour, are much worse" (135).

Liberty of Subjects:

- The liberty of man is consistent with the liberty from laws (covenants)—that is, the liberty of man to do whatever he wants to preserve his life if there is no commonwealth. Within the Commonwealth, liberty lies only in those things that, in regulating their actions, the Sovereign allows the Subjects to exercise, such as "the liberty to buy, and sell, and otherwise contract with one another; to choose their own abode, their own diet, their own trade of life, and institute their children as they themselves think fit, and the like." (138)

- The Sovereign has unlimited power over Subjects. "[N]othing the sovereign representative can do to a subject, on what pretence soever, can properly be called injustice, or injury, because every subject is author of every act the sovereign doth. . . ." (138)

- Liberty, which is praised by the Greeks and Romans, is liberty of the Sovereigns, not of private men (Subjects). For example, a commonwealth has the liberty to defend itself or invade other people, but the Subjects do not have the liberty to resist their own Sovereign. (139, 140)

- Subjects have limited liberty to disobey a Sovereign command. A subject is not bound to a Sovereign command to hurt himself, or to "kill, wound or maim himself, or not to resist those that assault him, or to abstain from the use of food, air, medicine or any other thing without which he cannot live. . . ." (142)
- Only in cases where the Sovereign has "prescribed no rule" may the Subject act or forbear at his own discretion. "And therefore such liberty is in some places more, and in some less, according as they that have the sovereignty shall think most convenient." (143)

Public Ministers are appointed by the Sovereign to represent him in the Commonwealth and to the Subjects. These Public Ministers have either general administrative authority or special administrative authority. They also have the authority to teach or enable others to teach, including instructing people as to what is just or unjust. Public Ministers are also the judges appointed by the Sovereign. They execute judgments, publish the Sovereign's commands, "suppress tumults," apprehend and imprison "malefactors," and generally act to preserve the peace. They also serve abroad to represent the Sovereign in all foreign matters. (155, 159)

"Distribution of Materials"

- The Sovereign assigns each man a parcel of land the size of which is determined by the Sovereign. The Commonwealth is also assigned a portion. (162, 163)
- The Sovereign controls all foreign trade and its distribution. (163)

- The Sovereign decides all laws for transferring property, including borrowing, buying, selling, exchanging, lending, letting, etc. (163)
- Using collectors, receivers, and treasurers the Sovereign controls the collection of money from the public and the dispersing of payments to the public. (164)

Only the "Commonwealth" can make laws. Whether the Sovereign is a monarch or an assembly of men, they legislate and only they can legislate (173). The Sovereign is not subject to the civil law, including written and unwritten laws (174, 175). All laws, written and unwritten, need interpretation, and their interpretation depends on the Sovereign and those he appoints (180).

Subjects are to be taught not to envy any form of government they observe in neighboring nations, for the success of the Commonwealth comes from the Subjects obeying the Sovereign. Any attempt to reform the Commonwealth will destroy it. Subjects are not to follow charismatic leaders or to dispute ("speak evil") of the Sovereign power (222, 223). Days are to be set apart for Subjects to attend assemblies to learn their duties to the Sovereign (223). Universities are to teach the youth and give instruction from the Sovereign (225, 226).

Those with strong bodies may not be idle; they are forced to work, with work provided by the Commonwealth. The poor but strong are sent to other countries not sufficiently inhabited to grow food in order to sustain themselves (228, 229).

For Hobbes, man in his natural state is out for himself. He must be prepared to fight, and in fact fight, to preserve himself and that which is his. And he has a right to all he claims, as does every other man. In such a natural state, there can be no justice or injustice. Therefore, man is in a constant state of war with man. In essence, Hobbes is describing anarchy.

Is anarchy, however, the true state of man in nature? Are there not occasions when man conducts himself honorably, morally, and civilly? Is man not also altruistic and compassionate? Do not most religions promote charity and selflessness? Moreover, even when acting in his self-interest, is it not in man's self-interest to coexist? Hobbes acknowledges that man is also inclined to pursue peace, but he insists his primary motivation is the fear of war. But experience proves time and again that man can and does work cooperatively and peacefully, where property rights and voluntary arrangements are respected and enforced, not out of trepidation but affirmative free will. Man is influenced by love, loyalty, logic, and a wide spectrum of interests, rationales, beliefs, and emotions. He develops customs and traditions that lend themselves to an orderly civil society. Of course, fear exists among men in the state of nature. And it is a legitimate motivating factor, but it is not necessarily paramount or exclusive. Indeed, is not an all-powerful Sovereign, which is Hobbes's answer, a greater and more certain threat to the individual?

Furthermore, if man in the state of nature is subjected to "continual fear and danger of violent death, and the life of man [is] solitary, poor, nasty, brutish, and short" (76), then why, as Hobbes insists, would men voluntarily unite and contract with each other to form a government? How can each trust the other to live up to his commitments and join together in a commonwealth?

Having united with each other Hobbes contends men will mutually transfer all their rights and liberties in the state of nature to a third party—that is, they will surrender the ability to govern themselves to the Sovereign, and primarily out of fear. But will they? And in the Leviathan, why would they? Although Hobbes insists that the Subjects will be treated equally under the law and their rights protected in a stable and secure society, the Sovereign—whether one person or an assembly of persons—possesses absolute power. He is not to be questioned or challenged in a way that might be perceived as weakening the Commonwealth. The Sovereign may also use terror and coercion to enforce the law, for the greatest fear is the potential for strife, conflict, and civil war. Consequently, the individual would be surrendering his rights and liberties to an all-powerful, centralized mastermind who Hobbes argues will behave prudently and judiciously—a benevolent dictator, if you will. Again, history suggests otherwise. Such regimes wield power in a manner that serves their own purposes, not the best interests of their Subjects. Is not the Sovereign to be feared? Moreover, it is difficult to reconcile Hobbes's distrust for the individual with his confidence in the altruistic nature of the individual or individuals who will oversee and control the Leviathan. Are not the latter also of flesh and blood? Hobbes seems to be saying that man's nature cannot be trusted but the nature of a ruler or a ruling assembly of men *can* be trusted. How so?

Hobbes creates a false choice between polar opposites. Either live in anarchy or live under despotism. He assumes most will choose despotism. Furthermore, once he surrenders his rights and liberties to the Sovereign, the individual has no way out unless his life is threatened. Is the Sovereign, who threatens the individual's life, going to be amenable to his disobedience or departure? Individuals are not drones. Hobbes acknowledges the obvious—that people reason, think, and learn. But in *Leviathan* he forbids even mild dissent. If tormented and abused by the all-powerful Sovereign, but without effective civil recourse, is it not possible—if not probable—that some portion of the population, dissatisfied and disaffected with their circumstances, will become radicalized, resist the Sovereign's rule, and even resort to violence in hopes of overthrowing him? If so, the peace and stability Hobbes promised would give way to the discord and conflicts he feared. In *Leviathan*, the Sovereign would be obliged to unleash all force necessary to protect the Commonwealth. Compromise or accommodation would seem out of the question, for the diminution of the Sovereign's absolute power would, in Hobbes's formulation, diminish the tranquility and survivability of the Commonwealth. As in the *Republic* and *Utopia*, absolute power over the individual requires a far-reaching police state.

For the individual, liberty exists only to the extent the Sovereign permits and only in those areas the Sovereign has not preempted with his own exercise of authority. "[A] free man is he that in those things which by his strength and wit he is able to do is not hindered to do what he has a will to do" (136). As in most tyrannies, the individual's liberty will undoubtedly and steadily constrict and erode. Such is the nature of absolute power in the hands of one man or a relative handful of men. For Hobbes, the individual must not be generally free to live his life as he sees fit, for his egoism knows no limits. In this regard, Hobbes shares More's mind-set in *Utopia*, in which More argues that the individual's pride deserves scorn and must be controlled by the central authority. But what of the individual's enlightened self-interest and ethical egoism—where, acting on his own behalf and in his own interest, he also benefits the greater society? Indeed, is this dynamic not vital to the functioning of a free and prosperous society?

Although Hobbes's discussion of economics and private property rights is not well developed, his relentless attack on individual self-interest, which he believes leads to greed and undermines the Commonwealth, combined with the assertion in *Leviathan* that the Subject has "the liberty to buy, and sell, and otherwise contract with one another; to choose their own abode, their own diet, their own trade of life, and institute their children as they themselves think fit, and the like" only to the extent the Sovereign allows, suggests the Sovereign will have the authority to control and appropriate whatever property he believes necessary and freely intervene in the individual's life decisions to ostensibly maintain the Commonwealth. Therefore, although the individual surrenders his rights and liberties to the Sovereign in exchange for protection and security, the Sovereign's priority is to safeguard himself. Obviously, throughout history unspeakable misery and violence have been perpetrated by tyrants in the name of the greater and common good.

Hobbes, like Plato and More, strips the individual of human qualities that contribute to the essence of life—motivation, inquisitiveness, competition, exploration, inventiveness, accomplishment, etc. Is not a society that cultivates individual initiative, independence, and self-sufficiency rather than discourages, suppresses, and punishes them likely to be a humane society? Conversely, rather than alleviating man's "continual fear and danger of violent death" and the miserable conditions that result in "the life of man" being "solitary, poor, nasty, brutish, and short," does not Hobbes design such a society? (76)

Hobbes also contends there cannot be morality or what he calls moral virtue—justice, gratitude, modesty, equity, mercy, etc.—in the state of nature, where man is in a constant state of war (100). Moral virtue can only exist in the framework of covenants among men as enforced in the broader social contract with the Sovereign. But it is inaccurate to argue that only covenants enforced by an all-powerful Sovereign promote or define moral virtue. Moral virtue, whether intuitive, learned, or reasoned, has preexisted the Commonwealth (or government). It has existed within families and among friends since the beginning of man. It has existed among the earliest trading partners and among native tribes. But just as immorality also preexisted the Commonwealth, men can covenant to do immoral things and governments can establish laws that lack moral justification or are executed in ways that promote immorality. It is simply inaccurate to insist that moral virtue is only possible and more likely under an all-powerful Sovereign.

From *Leviathan* springs not a virtuous government protective of the civil society but a totalitarian regime. As in Plato's *Republic* and More's *Utopia,* in *Leviathan* Hobbes rejects self-government because, he believes, the individual and man generally cannot be trusted to govern themselves. Hobbes designs another inhuman utopian structure that devours the individual.

CHAPTER FIVE

KARL MARX'S
COMMUNIST MANIFESTO AND
THE CLASS STRUGGLE

THE COMMUNIST MANIFESTO[1] WAS written by Karl Marx and Friedrich Engels in 1848 on behalf of the Communist League (although the final draft was Marx's). It set forth the historical and analytical bases for the international communist movement. The first sentence reads, "The history of all hitherto existing society is the history of class struggles." But unlike past class struggles, with their gradated class systems, "the modern bourgeois society that has sprouted from the ruins of feudal society, . . . has established new classes, new conditions of oppression, new forms of struggle in place of the old ones. . . ." Marx and Engels write, "Our epoch, the epoch of the bourgeois, possesses, however, this distinctive feature: it has simplified the class antagonisms. Society as a whole is more and more splitting up into two great hostile camps, into two great classes directly facing each other: Bourgeoisie [capitalists] and Proletariat [laborers]" (19).

For Marx and Engels, the market system may have destroyed feudalism, but it "left no other nexus between man and man than naked self-interest, callous 'cash payment.' . . . It has resolved personal worth into exchange value, and in place of the num-berless indefeasible chartered freedoms, has set up that single, unconscionable freedom—Free Trade. In one word, for exploita-tion, unveiled by religious and political illusions, it has substituted naked, shameless, direct, brutal exploitation. The bourgeoisie has stripped of its halo every occupation hitherto honored and looked up to with reverent awe. It has converted the physician, the law-yer, the priest, the poet, the man of science, into its paid wage laborers. The bourgeoisie has torn away from the family its senti-mental veil, and has reduced the family relation to a mere money relation" (20, 21).

What of economic advancement? Marx and Engels argue it is not advancement at all. "The bourgeoisie cannot exist without constantly revolutionizing the instruments of production, and thereby the relations of production, and with them the whole rela-tions of society. Conservation of the old modes of production in unaltered forms, was, on the contrary, the first condition of exis-tence for all earlier industrial classes. Constant revolutionizing of production, uninterrupted disturbance of all social conditions, ev-erlasting uncertainty and agitation, distinguish the bourgeois ep-och from all earlier ones. All fixed, fast-frozen relations, with their train of ancient and venerable prejudices and opinions, are swept away; all new-formed ones become antiquated before they can ossify. All that is solid melts into air, all that is holy is profaned, and man is at last compelled to face with sober senses his real conditions of life and his relations with his kind. The need of a constantly expanding market for its products chases the bourgeoisie over the whole surface of the globe. It must nestle everywhere, settle everywhere, establish connections everywhere" (21).

Therefore, the only just course is to eliminate the material wealth of the bourgeoisie. "In this sense the theory of Communists may be summed up in the single sentence: Abolition of private property. We Communists have been reproached with the desire of abolishing the right of personally acquiring property as the fruit of a man's own labor, which property is alleged to be the ground work of all personal freedom, activity and independence" (36). Yet, in wiping out the bourgeoisie's property are you not also eliminating that of the laborer? "But does wage labor create any property for the laborer? Not a bit. It creates capital, i.e., that kind of property which exploits wage labor, and which cannot increase except upon condition of begetting a new supply of wage-labor for fresh exploitation. Property, in its present form, is based on the antagonism of capital and wage labor" (36).

For Marx and Engels, it is crucial to sever all ties with the past, for the past is nothing more than a history of domination, in one form or another, over the proletariat. "In bourgeois society . . . the past dominates the present; in Communist society, the present dominates the past" (36). Unlike bourgeois society, where "living labor is but a means to increase accumulated labor, in Communist society accumulated labor is but a means to widen, to enrich, to promote the existence of the laborer" (37).

Marx and Engels argue that the accumulation of private property is unjust for it is nothing more than the taking of labor from those who earned it. "You're horrified at our intending to do away with private property. But in your existing society private property is already done away with for nine-tenths of the population; its existence for the few is solely due to its non-existence in the hands of those nine-tenths. You reproach us, therefore, with intending to do away with a form of property, the necessary condition for whose existence is the non-existence of any property for the immense majority of society. In one word, you reproach us with intending to do away with your property. Precisely so: that is just what we intend" (37, 38).

They also reject completely natural law and right reason as nothing more than the perpetuation of bourgeois control over the proletariat. "The selfish misconception that induces you to transform into eternal laws of nature and of reason, the social forms springing from your present mode of production and form of property—historical relations that rise and disappear in the progress of production—the misconception you share with every ruling class that has preceded you. What you see clearly in the case of ancient property, what you admit in the case of feudal property, you are of course forbidden to admit in the case of your own bourgeois form of property" (39).

Moreover, the family structure grew out of bourgeois material needs and must be dissolved for the good of the greater community. "Abolition of the family! Even the most radical flare up at this infamous proposal of the Communists. On what foundation is the present family, the bourgeois family, based? On capital, on private gain. In its completely developed form this family exists only among the bourgeoisie. But this state of things finds its complement in the practical absence of the family among the proletar-

ians, and in public prostitution. The bourgeois family will vanish
as a matter of course when its complement vanishes, and both will
vanish with the vanishing of capital. Do you charge us with want-
ing to stop the exploitation of children by their parents? To this
crime we plead guilty" (39).

Breaking from the past and family means breaking from tradition, customs, institutions, religion, and therefore requires that
communist indoctrination replace education. "But, you will say,
we destroy the most hallowed of relations, when we replace home
education by social. And your education! Is not that also social,
and determined by social conditions under which you educate,
by the intervention, direct or indirect, of society by means of
schools, etc.? The Communists have not invented the intervention of society in education; they do but seek to alter the character
of that intervention, and to rescue education from the influence
of the ruling class. The bourgeois clap-trap about the family and
education, about the hallowed co-relation of parent and child
become all the more disgusting, as, by the action of modern industry, all family ties among the proletarians are torn asunder,
and their children transformed into simple articles of commerce
and instruments of labor" (39, 40). "What else does the history
of ideas prove, than that intellectual production changes its
character in proportion as material production is changed? The
ruling ideas of each age have ever been the ideas of its ruling
class" (41).

Marx and Engels could not be clearer. "There are besides, eternal truths, such as Freedom, Justice, etc., that are common to all
states of society. But Communism abolishes eternal truths, it abolishes all religion and all morality, instead of constituting them on

a new basis; it therefore acts in contradiction to all past historical experience . . . The history of all past society has consisted in the development of class antagonisms that assumed different forms at different epochs" (41, 42).

All history, therefore, is the history of class struggle. "But whatever form they may have taken, one fact is common to all past ages—the exploitation of one part of society by the other. No wonder, then, that the social consciousness of past ages, despite all the multiplicity and variety it displays, moves within certain common forms, or general ideas, which cannot completely vanish except with the total disappearance of class antagonisms. The Communist revolution is the most radical rupture with traditional property relations; no wonder that its development involves the most radical rupture with traditional ideas" (42).

The proletariat will rise up in a working-class revolution and replace the bourgeois as the ruling class. It will "use its political supremacy to wrest, by degrees, all capital from the bourgeois; to centralize all instruments of production in the hands of the State, i.e., of the proletariat organized as the ruling class; and to increase the total of productive forces as rapidly as possible" (42).

Marx and Engels argue, almost as an aside, that "of course, in the beginning this cannot be effected except by despotic inroads on the rights of property and the conditions of bourgeois production." And they acknowledge that at least initially, there will be societal dislocation and misery. "[B]y means of measures, therefore, which appear economically insufficient and untenable, but which, in the course of the movement, outstrip themselves, necessitate further inroads upon the old social order and are unavoidable as a means of entirely revolutionizing the mode of production" (42).

Once the state is under the control of the proletariat, its objectives will generally include the following ten tenets (42, 43):

1. Abolition of property in land and application of all rents of land to public purposes
2. A heavy progressive or graduated income tax
3. Abolition of all right of inheritance
4. Centralization of the property of all emigrants and rebels
5. Centralization of credit in the hands of the state, by means of a national bank with state capital and an exclusive monopoly
6. Centralization of the means of communication and transport in the hands of the state
7. Extension of factories and instruments of production owned by the state; bringing into cultivation of waste lands, and the improvement of the soil generally in accordance with a common play
8. Equal liability of all to labor. Establishment of industrial armies, especially for agriculture.
9. Combination of agriculture with manufacturing industries; gradual abolition of the distinction between town and country, but a more equable distribution of the population over the country
10. Free education for all children in public schools. Abolition of children's factory labor in its present form. Combination of education with industrial production, etc.

After all remnants of bourgeois society are eliminated, having been replaced with a classless workers' paradise, the centralized, all-powerful state shall wither away. "When, in the course of development, class distinctions have disappeared and all production has been concentrated in the hands of a vast association of the whole nation, the public power will lose its political character. Political power, properly so called, is merely organized power of one class for oppressing another. If the proletariat during its contest with the bourgeois is compelled, by the force of circumstances, to organize itself in a class, if, by means of a revolution, it makes itself the ruling class, and as such, sweeps away by force the old conditions of production then it will, along with these conditions, have swept away the conditions for the existence of class antagonisms, and of classes generally, and will thereby have abolished its own supremacy as a class. In place of the old bourgeois society with its classes and class antagonisms we shall have an association in which the free development of each is the condition for the free development of all" (43, 44).

For Marx and Engels, their divination—that is, communism and the workers' paradise—is preordained. The history of man is a history of class struggle over materialism, where the feudal lords, landowners, and finally capitalists rule over the working class. Communism is the natural and final endpoint resulting from the motion of modern society. It is not an invention, discovery, or reform; its ultimate certainty cannot be obstructed by law or politics. It is the truth (35). Not only would Marx and Engels denounce any attempt to label their fantasy a utopia, but in *The Communist Manifesto* they are extremely critical of what they call Utopian Socialism and Communism. "[A]s the modern class struggle develops and takes definite shape, this phantastic standing apart from the contest, these phantastic attacks on it lose all practical value and all theoretical justification. . . . They therefore, endeavor, and that consistently, to deaden the class struggle and to reconcile the class antagonisms. They still dream of their experimental realization of their social Utopias . . . they are compelled to appeal to the feelings and purses of the bourgeois. By degrees they sink into the category of the reactionary socialists. . . ." (57) As such, only a complete break from the past and a cleansing of modern society can set the stage for the classless state, where there would be no need for politics or government. They insist there can be no compromise with bourgeois history or standards. There can be no remnants of what was and is.

However, in their denunciation of Utopian Socialism and Communism as "violently oppos[ing] all political action on the part of the working class," Marx and Engels demonstrate the fanaticism of their utopianism (57, 58). After all, the half measures expose communism as not inevitable but impracticable and impossible. It is one thing to espouse views about man's historic class and economic struggles and predict the future—the inevitable workers' revolution leading to an ultimate egalitarian nirvana. It is another to make the fantasy tangible and develop the institutions and mechanics to institute it. As Karl Popper noted, Vladmir "Lenin was quick to realize [that] Marxism was unable to help in matters of practical economics. 'I do not know of any socialist who has dealt with these problems . . . there was nothing written about such matters in the Bolshevik textbooks, or in those of the Mensheviks.'. . . As Lenin admits, *there is hardly a word on the economics of socialism to be found in Marx's work. . . .*' "[2]

Man's nature and history are not neatly defined through economic classes, whose members are easily categorized. To say that man exists in essentially one of two conditions—a bourgeois or capitalist/

landlord class or a proletariat or working class, with the former perpetually exploiting the latter and the latter perpetually exploited
by the former—is simply erroneous. French philosopher Raymond
Aron observed half a century ago, "To declare flatly that a worker
in a capitalist factory in France or the United States is by definition exploited and that a worker in a Soviet factory is not, is not
an example of synthetic thought, it is pure nonsense. It is merely a
convenient way of substituting verbal gymnastics for a painstaking
investigation of reality."[3] Moreover, as I discussed in *Liberty and
Tyranny,* applying this notion to American society makes obvious its incoherence. "[W]ho populates this [working class]? Is the
twenty-five-year-old female paralegal who graduated from college,
works at a large law firm, earns $85,000 a year, is unmarried and
without children, lives in an apartment in Manhattan, and rarely
attends church in the same [working class] as the fifty-seven-year-
old male auto mechanic who did not graduate from high school,
works at Pep Boys, earns $55,000 a year, lives in a row home in
northeast Philadelphia, is married with four children, and attends
church every Sunday?"[4]

In an absurd attempt to address the obvious fallacy of their
post-feudalism, two-class construct, Marx and Engels describe
bourgeois and proletariat subclasses, such as the petty bourgeois
and weaker capitalists, who may even become wage earners, as
well as the lower strata of the so-called middle class, including
shopkeepers and tradesmen, etc. They are said to ultimately transition into the proletariat. As the subclasses increase the number
of proletarians, bourgeois wealth increases and capital becomes
more concentrated in fewer individuals. The proletarians work
harder and become poorer.

Meanwhile, the never-ending capitalist pursuit of new technologies further impoverishes the proletariat. Eventually the middle class disappears, the proletariat rises up, and the bourgeois is vanquished—violently if necessary. Afterward, society is ruled by a dictatorship of the proletariat, which creates the conditions for the classless society. At some point, Marx and Engels predict, the state withers away. What is left is "an association in which the free development of each is the condition for the free development of all" (43).

The likelihood that the ruling proletariat might break into factions and internal power struggles, with would-be masterminds competing for control over the society; or that it might spawn additional subclasses; or that once in a position to exercise absolute power a dictator or supreme party would voluntarily surrender their power and wither away, are not even addressed in *The Communist Manifesto*. To have done so, however, would have required Marx and Engels to once again acknowledge the hopelessness of their utopia. But this is the history and nature of communist governments. In the end, they are totalitarian regimes. What withers away are individual liberties and rights.

The impact of Marx and Engels on mankind has been enormous and devastating. Notwithstanding one hundred years of communist tyranny and mass genocide, the fanatics cling to their utopia. Any failure is in man and the men who bastardize communism—Joseph Stalin, Mao Zedong, Fidel Castro, et al.— not in the dogma. True communism, they argue, has never been faithfully executed. After all, as Marx and Engels preached, the workers' paradise is inevitable.

The two-class economic construct, with one class of people perpetually victimizing another class of people, is both crude and defective. The history of man and the nature of individuals are more complex than the simplistic materialist construct of communism and its radical egalitarianism. Yet Marx and Engels invented them and assigned them more value than the individual, ensuring communism's inhumanity. There is infinite diversity among the individuals within the so-called bourgeois and proletariat—not only economic but religious, social, geographical, political, etc. There are also differences in character traits among individuals—psychological, emotional, intellectual, moral, etc. Moreover, some degree of disunity among individuals within the classes would be natural, as would some degree of harmony and cooperation between individuals in the two classes. In the end, however, when and how are we to know when material equality has been achieved? How is it actually defined and measured and by whom?

As for Marx and Engels's condemnation of capitalism, industrialization through capitalism would lead to economic progress that improved the lifestyles of tens of millions in Europe and North America. Advances were made in manufacturing, transportation, agriculture, technology, etc. New products and services improved upon existing ones. New skills were learned as new job opportunities became available. For most, their standard of living improved as they earned more and their material needs and wants became more affordable. In America, automobiles, homes or apartments, running water, flush toilets, electricity, refrigerators, freezers, ovens, stoves, microwaves, air-conditioning, washing machines, dryers, televisions, telephones, etc. are commonplace. More wealth and opportunity have been created by and for more people than under any other economic model. In fact, rather than emancipate themselves from the system, the so-called proletariat helped shape it, benefit from it, contribute to it, and fight wars to defend it. The market system is imperfect, but it is the most perfect of economic systems.

The proletarians never rose up to overthrow their capitalist systems. Nor did they join together across national boundaries in a global revolution. They clearly rejected Marx's rallying cry— "Workers of the world, unite!" (64) In fact, in 1989 in Poland, the communist regime was driven from power by popular strikes and protests led by Lech Walesa, leader of the anti-Soviet Solidarity union, among others. Soon Hungary, East Germany, Bulgaria, Czechoslovakia, and Romania would follow. In 1991, the Soviet Union itself collapsed, resulting in more countries throwing off communism. A form of autocratic pseudo-capitalism has been adopted in China, lest its people starve as in neighboring North Korea. Marx was also wrong when he predicted that larger and larger industrial enterprises would consume so much available capital that they would crowd out smaller businesses. In America, small businesses are vital to the economy. In 2010, 98.2 percent of businesses had fewer than 100 employees, 89.3 percent had fewer than 20 employees, 78.6 percent had fewer than 10 employees, and 60.8 percent had fewer than 5 employees.[5]

Having dealt briefly but adequately with Marx-Engels's "prophecy," what of historic materialism—that is, the proposition, generally stated, that history can only or primarily be viewed through the lens of material class struggle? Of course, economics and materialism have played a significant role in the course of history, but so have religion, war, nationalism, law, and politics. In some societies, they have been and are inextricably linked; in others, less so. The demarcations are not always evident or uncomplicated. Missing from The Communist Manifesto's flawed arguments are the inalienable rights of the individual. Man is dehumanized and his actual identity is lost in the communist utopia. If he is "wealthy," such as a landowner, business owner, or landlord, he is part of an evil group, whether he is evil or not. If he does not divest himself of his wealth, it will be confiscated from him, by force if necessary. If he is "not wealthy" or a laborer, he is part of a good group, whether he is good or not. Only the latter group survives. The individual's fate is sealed by a fiction based largely on an economic classification assigned to him by political philosophers and, in the end, a workers' paradise that is said to be inevitable.

This approach of predestined pigeonholing of the individual is closer to the utopias in the *Republic*, *Utopia*, and *Leviathan* than may appear on the surface. First, some of the distinctions: The *Republic*, *Utopia*, and *Leviathan* are top-down tyrannies, with wisdom concentrated among a handful of rulers—the omnipotent philosopher-king, the Prince, and the Sovereign, respectively; Marx and Engels describe their communist utopia as a bottom-up economic liberation movement in which "the people" become the rulers as a requisite to the state withering away. The *Republic*, *Utopia*, and *Leviathan* are not only grandiose ideals, but their authors also describe in mind-numbing detail the mechanics of their societies; Marx and Engels avoid the mechanics almost completely and condemn those who try to develop them, concentrating almost exclusively on the supposed historical, material, and political case for their dogma and its inescapability.

In all four utopias, the individual and his family are subservient to the state. Society, however, would be a far better place if only man would change his nature to accommodate the utopian ideal. Since, left to his own devices, man will not oblige, he must be made to do so. Yet out of this same riffraff, the masterminds are born—both the revolutionaries and the rulers. They rise above "the masses" for, unlike the rest, they are self-evidently altruistic, prudent, virtuous, and wise. Whether or not they know how to run their own lives, they know how to run the lives of others. Of course, the entire enterprise is immoral if not deranged.

The Communist Manifesto seethes with hate for the so-called bourgeoisie. Their freedom, families, and of course, property, must all be abolished. "This person must, indeed, be swept out of the way and made impossible" (38). "Abolition of the family! Even the most radical flare up at this infamous proposal of the Communists" (39). "In this sense the theory of Communism may be summed up in the single sentence: Abolition of private property" (36). "The proletariat will use its political supremacy to wrest, by degrees, all capital from the bourgeoisie. . . ." (42) "[I]n the beginning this cannot be effected except by means of despotic inroads on the rights of property and on the conditions of bourgeois production. . . ." (42) However, the whole of society suffers at the masterminds' hands, for in its purest form, communism demands a radical egalitarianism best described as an absolute equality of social conditions and an exactness of burdens and benefits. The entire society must be brought down to its lowest level. Individual sovereignty must be wrung from the human character; everyone becomes a slave to the state and there is no escape for anyone, including the vaunted and fabled proletarian. In every instance, communism requires the establishment of a police state, some more violent than others, because this utopia, like the others described earlier, is not only undesirable but impossible—and its pursuit is merciless and relentless.

Despite this record, communism's utopian underpinnings and characteristics attract sympathetic attention, including in America and especially among the intelligentsia and malcontented, as it is romanticized as "social justice" and a "liberation" movement. Writing of these sympathizers, Aron observed, "Not only are they sacrificing the best part of the legacy of the Enlightenment— respect for reason, liberalism—but they are sacrificing it in an age when there is no reason for the sacrifice, at least in the West . . ."[6]

PART II

ON AMERICANISM

CHAPTER SIX

JOHN LOCKE AND THE
NATURE OF MAN

JOHN LOCKE, WHO LIVED from 1632 to 1704, had an enormous influence on the American founding and, consequently, American society. As will become clear, he did not seek ways to destroy the sovereignty of the individual; he sought to understand and cultivate it. Unlike the utopians, who build insensate societies based on their own prejudices and fantasies, Locke explored the true nature of man, including his acquisition of knowledge and use of intuition, reason, and sensation. It is not necessary to agree with all of Locke's conclusions to celebrate his extraordinary insight.

In *An Essay Concerning Human Understanding*[1] (published in 1690), which is an extensive examination of the capacity of the human mind, including its limits—Locke dramatically distinguished his philosophical approach from the utopians. He explained: "Since it is the Understanding that sets Man above the rest of sensible Beings, and gives him all the Advantage and Dominion, which he has over them; it is certainly a Subject, even for its Nobleness, worth our Labour to enquire into. The Understanding, like the Eye, whilst it makes us see, and perceive all other Things, takes not notice of it self: And it requires Art and Pains to set it at a distance, and make it its own Object. But whatever be the Difficulties, that lie in the way of this Enquiry; whatever it be, that keeps us so much in the Dark to our selves; sure I am, that all the Light we can let in upon our own Minds; all the Acquaintance we can make with our own Understandings, will not only be very pleasant; but bring us great Advantage, in directing our Thoughts in search of other Things" (I, 1, 1).

For Locke, the individual has value, dignity, and significance. Rather than advance a dogma in search of a fantasy, Locke believed that the individual's mind was worth exploring. As if lecturing the utopians, Locke wrote, "When we know our own Strength, we shall the better know what to undertake with hopes of Success: And when we have well survey'd the Powers of our own Minds, and made some Estimate what we may expect from them, we shall not be inclined either to sit still, and not set our Thoughts on work at all, in Despair of knowing any thing; nor on the other side question every thing, and disclaim all Knowledge, because some Things are not to be understood. . . ." (I, 1, 6)

"I thought that the first Step towards satisfying the several Enquiries, the Mind of Man was apt to run into, was, to take a Survey of our own Understandings, examine our own Powers, and see to what Things they were adapted. Till that was done, I suspected that we began at the wrong end, and in vain sought for Satisfaction in a quiet and secure Possession of Truths, that most concern'd us whilst we let loose our Thoughts into the vast Ocean of *Being*, as if all the boundless Extent, were the natural and undoubted Possessions of our Understandings, wherein there was nothing that escaped its Decisions, or that escaped its Comprehension. Thus Men, extending their Enquiries beyond their Capacities, and letting their Thoughts wander into the depths where they can find no sure Footing; 'tis no Wonder, that they raise Questions and multiply Disputes, which never coming to any clear Resolution, are proper to only continue and increase their Doubts, and to confirm them at last in a perfect Skepticism. Whereas were the Capacities of our Understanding well considered, the Extent of our Knowledge once discovered, and the Horizon found, which sets the boundary between the enlightened and the dark Parts of things; between what is and what is not comprehensible by us, Men would perhaps with less scruple acquiesce in the avow'd Ignorance of the one; and employ their Thoughts and Discourse, with more Advantage and Satisfaction in the other" (I, 1, 7).

Locke found that experience, uncovered through observation and right reason, is decisive to comprehending man. "Let us then suppose the Mind to be, as we say, white Paper, void of all Characters, without any *Ideas*. How comes it to be furnished? Whence comes it by that vast store, which the busy and boundless Fancy of Man has painted on it, with an almost endless variety? Whence has it all the materials of Reason and Knowledge? To this I answer, in one word, From *Experience*. In that, all our Knowledge is founded; and from that it ultimately derives it self. Our Observation employ'd either about *external, sensible Objects; or about the internal Operations of our Minds, perceived and reflected on by our selves, is that, which supplies our Understandings with all the materials of thinking.* These two are the Fountains of Knowledge, from whence all the *Ideas* we have, or can naturally have do spring" (II, 1, 2).

Locke carried forward his scrutiny of man's understanding with an anti-authoritarian approach to the civil society and governance. As if explicitly rejecting Thomas Hobbes's view of human nature, where in the state of nature man is in perpetual fear and society must rely on an all-powerful sovereign for security, in *The Second Treatise of Government*[2] (composed between 1685 and 1688), Locke asserts, "so that he that will not give just occasion to think that all government in the world is the product only of force and violence, and that men live together by no other rules but that of beasts, where the strongest carries it, and so lay a foundation for perpetual disorder and mischief, tumult, sedition, and rebellion (things that the followers of that hypothesis so loudly cry out against), must of necessity find out another rise of government, another original of political power. . . ." (1, 1)

Indeed, Locke took the view opposite of Hobbes's. He argued, "To understand political power right, and derive it from its original, we must consider, what state all men are naturally in, and that is, a state of perfect freedom to order their actions, and dispose of their possessions and persons, as they think fit, within the bounds of the law of nature, without asking leave, or depending upon the will of any other man. A state also of equality, wherein all the power and jurisdiction is reciprocal, no one having more than another; there being nothing more evident, than that creatures of the same species and rank, promiscuously born to all the same advantages of nature, and the use of the same faculties, should also be equal one amongst another without subordination or subjection, unless the lord and master of them all should, by any manifest declaration of his will, set one above another, and confer on him, by an evident and clear appointment, an undoubted right to dominion and sovereignty" (2, 4). "This equality of men by nature . . . makes it the foundation of that obligation to mutual love amongst men, on which he builds the duties they owe one another, and from whence he derives the great maxims of justice and charity" (2, 5).

By equality, Locke does not mean equality of outcomes or result. He does not mean conformity. Early in *The Second Treatise of Government,* Locke introduces the notion of the individual's God-given inalienable rights, of which all individuals are entitled, and which provide the moral condition for civil society. "The state of Nature has a law of Nature to govern it, which obliges everyone, and reason, which is that law, teaches all mankind who will but consult it, that being all equal and independent, no one ought to harm another in his life, health, liberty or possessions; for men being all the workmanship of one omnipotent and infinitely wise Maker; all the servants of one sovereign Master, sent into the world by His order and about His business; they are His property, whose workmanship they are made to last during His, not one another's pleasure. And being furnished with like faculties, sharing all in one community of Nature, there cannot be supposed any such subordination among us that may authorize us to destroy one another, as if we were made for one another's uses, as the inferior ranks of creatures are for ours. Everyone as he is bound to preserve himself, and not to quit his station willfully, so by the like reason, when his own preservation comes not in competition, ought he as much as he can to preserve the rest of mankind, and not unless it be to do justice on an offender, take away or impair the life or what tends to the preservation of the life, the liberty, health, limb, or goods of another" (2, 6). Thus, individual sovereignty, for one and all, is the key to understanding, accepting, and preserving the natural state of man and the civil society.

Unlike Hobbes, Locke observed that men generally get along with each other in the state of nature, for their own sake and the sake of the community, although it is certainly not perfect. A state of war exists in the state of nature only when one individual violates the laws of nature—that is, the inalienable rights of another. "In transgressing the law of Nature, the offender declares himself to live by another rule than that of reason and common equity, which is that measure God has set to the actions of men for their mutual security, and so he becomes dangerous to mankind. . . ." (2, 8)

Therefore, although the state of nature is not the violent, fearful condition that Hobbes described, the laws of nature are and can be violated. Moreover, the individual has the right to enforce the laws of nature against those who violate his rights and to assist others whose rights have been violated. The perpetrators are said to be committing acts of war against the society. "And in this case, and upon this ground, every man hath a right to punish the offender, and be executioner of the law of Nature" (2, 8). But Locke also observes that this can lead to injustices, since those enforcing their rights are not impartial. "[S]elf-love will make men partial to themselves and their friends; and, on the other side, ill-nature, passion, and revenge will carry them too far in punishing others, and hence nothing but confusion and disorder will follow, and that therefore God has certainly appointed government to restrain the partiality and violence of men. I easily grant that civil government is the proper remedy for the inconveniences of the state of Nature. . . ." (2, 13)

Locke makes the case for a civil and consensual government with just laws impartially enforced and in which the liberty and rights of the individual are respected, thereby rejecting the utopian centralized model where the philosopher-king, prince, sovereign, or "temporary" despot rules over "the masses" and shapes the individual against his will. Locke wrote, "The Natural liberty of man is to be free from any superior power on earth, and not to be under the will or legislative authority of man, but to have only the law of Nature for his rule. The liberty of man in society is to be under no legislative power but that established by consent in the commonwealth, nor under the domination of any will, restraint of any law, but what that legislative shall enact according to the trust put in it. . . . [F]reedom of men under government is to have a standing rule to live by, common to everyone of that society, and made by the legislative power erected in it. A liberty to follow my own will in all things where the rule prescribes not, not to be subject to the inconstant, uncertain, unknown, arbitrary will of another man, as freedom of nature is to be under no other restraint but the law of Nature" (4, 21). "This freedom from absolute, arbitrary power is so necessary to, and closely joined with, a man's preservation, that he cannot part with it but by what forfeits his preservation and life together. For a man, not having the power of his own life, cannot by compact or his own consent enslave himself to anyone, nor put himself under the absolute, arbitrary power of another to take away his life when he pleases. Nobody can give more power than he has himself, and he that cannot take away his own life cannot give that power over it" (4, 22).

Locke further distinguishes himself by asserting not only the individual's fundamental right to private property but also the government's obligation to respect and uphold that right, for it is central to the sovereignty of the individual. He describes the nature of labor and property in the state of nature, the transition from bartering to the use of money, and what is, in essence, the societal vitality of the market system. Locke explains that in the state of nature, "The earth and all that is therein is given to men for the support and comfort of their being. And though all the fruits it naturally produces, and beasts it feeds, belong to mankind in common, as they are produced by the spontaneous hand of Nature, and nobody has originally a private dominion exclusive of the rest of mankind in any of them, as they are thus in their natural state, yet being given for the use of men, there must of necessity be a means to appropriate them some way or other before they can be of any use, or at all beneficial, to any particular men. . . ." (5, 25) "Though the earth and all inferior creatures be common to all men, yet every man has a 'property' in his own 'person.' This nobody has any right to but himself. The 'labor' of his body and the 'work' of his hands, we may say, are properly his. Whatsoever, then, he removes out of the state that Nature hath provided and left it in, he hath mixed his labor with, and joined to it something that is his own, and thereby makes it his property. It being by him removed from the common state Nature hath placed it in, it hath by his labor something annexed to it that excludes the common right of other men. For this 'labor' being the unquestionable property of the laborer, no man but he can have a right to what that is once joined to, at least where there is enough, and as good left in common for others" (5, 16).

For Locke, labor represents initiative, productivity, and enterprise, which are imperative to not only the survival of the individual but also his well-being and success. "As much land as a man tills, plants, improves, cultivates, and can use the product of, so much is his property. He by his labor does, as it were, enclose it from the common. . . . God, when He gave the world in common to all mankind, commanded man also to labor, and the penury of his condition required it of him. God and his reason commanded him to subdue the earth—i.e., improve it for the benefit of life and therein lay out something upon it that was his own, his labor. He that, in obedience to this command of God, subdued, tilled, and sowed any part of it, thereby annexed to it something that was his property, which another had not title to, nor could without injury take from him" (5, 31). Moreover, Locke explained that the wealth created and possessed by one individual does not prevent another individual from creating and possessing wealth. "Nor was this appropriation of any parcel of land, by improving it, any prejudice to any other man, since there was still enough and as good left, and more than the yet unprovided could use. So that, in effect, there was never the less left for others because of his enclosure for himself. For he that leaves as much as another can make use of does as good as take nothing at all. Nobody could think himself injured by the drinking of another man, though he took a good draught, who had a whole river of the same water left him to quench his thirst. . . ." (5, 32)

Indeed, Locke explained that the individual's productive labor improves the entire society. "Nor is it so strange as, perhaps, before consideration, it may appear, that the property of labor should be able to overbalance the community of land, for it is labor indeed that puts the difference of value on everything; and let anyone consider what the difference is between an acre of land planted with tobacco or sugar, sown with wheat or barley, and an acre of the same land lying in common without any husbandry upon it, and he will find that the improvement of labor makes the far greater part of the value. I think it will be but a very modest computation to say, that of the products of the earth useful to the life of man, nine-tenths are the effects of labor. Nay, if we will rightly estimate things as they come to our use, and cast up the several expenses about them—what in them is purely owing to Nature and what to labor—we shall find that in most of them ninety-nine hundredths are wholly to be put on the account of labor" (5, 40).

Locke also reproves the apathetic, lethargic, and envious against interfering with and making demands on the conscientious and hardworking, for they have not contributed to their own well-being or that of society. "God gave the world to men in common, but since He gave it them for their benefit and the greatest conveniences of life they were capable to draw from it, it cannot be supposed He meant it should always remain common and uncultivated. He gave it to the use of the industrious and rational (and labor was to be his title to it); not to the fancy or covetousness of the quarrelsome and contentious. He that has as good left for his improvement as was already taken up needed not complain, ought not to meddle with what was already improved by another's labor. If he did, it is plain he desired the benefit of another's pains, which he had no right to, and not the ground which God had given him, in common with others, to labor on, and whereof there was as good left as that already possessed, and more than he knew what to do with, or his industry could reach to" (5, 33). Clearly, therefore, Locke's notion of equality diverges fundamentally from the utopians' radical egalitarianism.

Locke described the natural evolution and rational behavior of man in commerce. "The greatest part of things really useful to the life of man, and such as the necessity of subsisting made the first commoners of the world look after—as it doth the Americans now—are generally things of short duration, such as—if they are not consumed by use—will decay and perish of themselves. Gold, silver, and diamonds are things that fancy or agreement hath put the value on, more than real use and the necessary support of life. Now of those good things which Nature hath provided in common, everyone hath a right (as hath been said) to as much as he could use, and had a property in all he could effect with his labor; all that his industry could extend to, to alter from the state Nature had put it in, was his. He that gathered a hundred bushels of acorns or apples had thereby a property in them; they were his goods as soon as gathered. He was only to look that he used them before they spoiled, else he took more than his share, and robbed others. And, indeed, it was a foolish thing, as well as dishonest, to hoard up more than he could make use of. If he gave away a part to anybody else, so that it perished not uselessly in his possession, these he also made use of. And if he also bartered away plums that would have rotted in a week, for nuts that would last good for his eating a whole year, he did no injury; he wasted not the common stock; destroyed no part of the portion of goods that belonged to others, so long as nothing perished uselessly in his hands. Again, if he would give his nuts for a piece of metal, pleased with its color, or exchange his sheep for shells, or wool for a sparkling pebble or a diamond, and keep those by him all his life, he invaded not the right of others; he might heap up as much of these durable things as he pleased; the exceeding of the bounds of his just property not lying in the largeness of his possession, but the perishing of anything uselessly in it" (5, 46).

As money replaced barter, the individual was able to acquire more than he needed for his immediate use or consumption—that is, he could accumulate assets, make longer-term investments, save and better plan for his future, and pass his wealth on to future generations. "And thus came in the use of money; some lasting thing that men might keep without spoiling, and that, by mutual consent, men would take in exchange for the truly useful but perishable supports of life" (5, 47). Moreover, there could never be equality of economic outcomes. "And as different degrees of industry were apt to give men possessions in different proportions, so this invention of money gave them the opportunity to continue and enlarge them" (5, 48). "But since gold and silver, being little useful to the life of man, in proportion to food, raiment, and carriage, has its value only from the consent of men—whereof labor yet makes in great part the portionate and unequal possession of the earth—I mean out of the bounds of society and compact; for in governments the laws regulate it; they having, by consent, found out and agreed in a way how a man may, rightfully and without injury, possess more than he himself can make use of by receiving gold and silver, which may continue long in a man's possession without decaying for the overplus, and agreeing those metals should have a value" (5, 50).

Locke emphasized that the right to acquire and retain property is inextricably linked to man's liberty. In the state of nature, the individual is justified in enforcing that right against transgressors. "Man being born . . . with a title to perfect freedom and an uncontrolled enjoyment of all the rights and privileges of the law of Nature, equally with any other man, or number of men in the world, hath by nature a power not only to preserve his property—that is, his life, liberty, and estate, against the injuries and attempts of other men, but to judge of and punish the breaches of that law in others, as he is persuaded the offense deserves, even with death itself, in crimes where the heinousness of the fact, in his opinion, requires it. . . ." (7, 87)

Government is established, with the consent of the members of society, to protect the individual's liberty and the order of society, in particular property rights, through just and predictable laws and their impartial enforcement. "Those who are united into one body, and have a common established law and judicature to appeal to, with authority to decide controversies between them and punish offenders, are in civil society one with another. . . ." (7, 87) "And thus the commonwealth comes by a power to set down what punishment shall belong to the several transgressions they think worthy of it, committed amongst the members of that society (which is the power of making laws), as well as it has the power to punish any injury unto any of its members by anyone that is not of it (which is the power of war and peace); and all this for the preservation of the property of all the members of that society, as far as is possible" (7, 88).

But the wrong government—a centralized authority of one or more rulers—is destructive of the individual's liberty and the civil society. "For he being supposed to have all, both legislative and executive, power in himself alone, there is no judge to be found, no appeal lies open to anyone, who may fairly and indifferently, and with authority decide, and from whence relief and redress may be expected of any injury or inconveniency that may be suffered from him, or by his order. . . . That whereas, in the ordinary state of Nature, he has a liberty to judge of his right, according to the best of his power to maintain; but whenever his property is invaded by the will and order of his monarch, he has not only no appeal, as those in society ought to have, but, as if he were degraded from the common state of rational creatures, is denied a liberty to judge of, or defend his right, and so is exposed to all the misery and inconveniences that a man can fear from one, who being in the unrestrained state of Nature, is yet corrupted with flattery and armed with power" (7, 91). "For he that thinks absolute power purifies men's blood, and corrects the baseness of human nature, need read but the history of this, or any other age, to be convinced to the contrary" (7, 92). Locke is not only repudiating Hobbes's notion of an omnipotent Sovereign, but the philosopher-kings in Plato's *Republic*.

Locke argued for a representative government but warned that it, too, required restraints, for all forms of government are self-perpetuating. "The great end of men's entering into society being the enjoyment of their properties in peace and safety, and the great instrument and means of that being the laws established in that society, the first and fundamental positive law of all commonwealths is the establishing of the legislative power, as the first and fundamental natural law which is to govern even the legislative" (11, 134). The legislative power "is a power that hath no other end but preservation, and therefore can never have a right to destroy, enslave, or designedly to impoverish the subjects. . . ." (11, 135)

Morever, the legislature has as its task to uphold and secure man's inalienable rights, be informed by the governed, be free of corruption, and constrain itself. "Thus the law of Nature stands as an eternal rule to all men, legislators as well as others. The rules that they make for other men's actions must, as well as their own and other men's actions, be comfortable to the law of Nature— i.e., to the will of God, of which that is a declaration, and the fundamental law of Nature being the preservation of mankind, no human sanction can be good or valid against it" (11, 135). "These are the bounds which the trust is put in them by the society and the law of God and Nature have set to the legislative power of every commonwealth, in all forms of government. First: They are to govern by promulgated established laws, not to be varied in particular cases, but to have one rule for rich and poor, for the favorite at Court, and the countryman at plough. Secondly: These laws also ought to be designed for no other end ultimately but the good of the people. Thirdly: They must not raise taxes on the property of the people without the consent of the people given by themselves or their deputies. . . . Fourthly: Legislative neither must nor can transfer the power of making laws to anybody else, or place it anywhere but where the people have" (11, 142).

Locke explains the necessity of an executive to carry out the laws adopted by the legislature "because those laws which are constantly to be executed, and whose force is always to continue, may be made in a little time, therefore there is no need that the legislative should be always in being, not having always business to do. And because it may be too great temptation to human frailty, apt to grasp at power, for the same persons who have the power of making laws to have also in their hands the power to execute them. . . ." (12, 143) Hence, Locke makes clear the distinction between the executive enforcing legislative acts and the usurpation of the legislature and the people by the delegation of lawmaking authority to other entities.

Locke also argues for the impartial adjudication of disputes as a compelling reason for the acceptance of consensual government. He wrote, "Firstly, there wants an established, settled, known law, received and allowed by common consent to be the standard of right and wrong, and the common measure to decide all controversies between them. . . ." (9, 124) "Secondly, in the state of Nature there wants a known and indifferent judge, with authority to determine all differences according to the established law. . . ." "And so whoever has the legislative or supreme power of any common-wealth, is bound to govern by established standing laws, promulgated and known to the people, and not by extemporary decrees; by indifferent and upright judges, who are to decide controversies by those laws" (9, 131).

Consequently, Locke argues that the only legitimate form of government is that which is established by the consent of the members of society; that the only kind of government that can preserve the individual's God-given natural rights, including his liberty and labor/property, is a representative commonwealth in which there are three branches or at least three distinct responsibilities; that it must operate through just and impartial laws, which are applied equally to everyone in the society, including those in government; and that the extraordinary power of making laws must not be delegated to those who are beyond the reach of the governed.

However, if the government loses its legitimate purpose, its form is irrelevant. "As usurpation is the exercise of power which another hath a right to, so tyranny is the exercise of power beyond right, which nobody can have a right to; and this is making use of the power anyone has in his hands, not for the good of those who are under it, but for his own private, separate advantage. When the governor, however entitled, makes not the law, but his will, the rule; and his commands and actions are not directed to the preservation of the properties of his people, but the satisfaction of his own ambition, revenge, covetousness, or any other irregular passion" (18, 199).

Locke emphasized that even representative governments, of the kind he described, can take on a tyrannical character. "It is a mistake to think that fault is proper only to monarchies. Other forms of government are liable to it as well as that; for wherever the power that is put in any hands for the government of the people and the preservation of their properties is applied to other ends, and made use of to impoverish, harass, or subdue them to the arbitrary and irregular commands of those that have it, there it presently becomes tyranny, whether those that thus use it are one or many" (18, 201).

Should government turn tyrannical, discarding its original purpose, it ceases to be legitimate. Locke declares, "The reason why men enter into society is the preservation of their property; and the end while they choose and authorize a legislative is that there may be laws made, and rules set, as guards and fences to the properties of all the society, to limit the power and moderate the dominion of every part and member of the society. For since it can never be supposed to be the will of the society that the legislative should have a power to destroy that which everyone designs to secure by entering into society, and for which the people submitted themselves to legislators of their own making; whenever the legislators endeavour to take away and destroy the property of the people, or to reduce them to slavery under arbitrary power, they put themselves into a state of war with the people, who are thereupon absolved from any farther obedience, and are left to the common refuge which God hath provided for all men against force and violence." In such circumstances "the people, who have a right to resume their original liberty, and by the establishment of a new legislative (such as they shall think fit), provide for their own safety and security, which is the end for which they are in society. . . . What I have said here concerning the legislative in general holds true also concerning the [executive]. . . ." (19, 222)

Locke also insisted that the right to revolt is not to be exercised imprudently. "[S]uch revolutions happen not upon every little mismanagement in public affairs. Great mistakes in the ruling part, many wrong and inconvenient laws, and all the slips of human frailty will be borne by the people without mutiny or murmur. But if a long train of abuses, prevarications, and artifices, all tending the same way, make the design visible to people, and they cannot but feel what they lie under, and see whither they are going, it is not to be wondered that they should then rouse themselves, and endeavour to put the rule into such hands which may secure to them the ends for which government was first erected, and without which, ancient names and specious forms are so far from being better, that they are much worse than the state of Nature or pure anarchy; the inconveniences being all as great and as near, but the remedy farther off and more difficult" (19, 225).

"But if they have set limits to the duration of their legislative, and made this supreme power in any person or assembly only temporary; or else when by the miscarriages of those in authority, it is forfeited; upon the forfeiture of their rulers, or the determination of the time set, it reverts to the society, and the people have a right to act as supreme, and continue the legislative in themselves or place it in a new form, or new hands, as they think good" (19, 243).

Locke would undoubtedly consider the modern-day political declarations about "spreading the wealth" or "redistributing the wealth" or "leveling the playing field," and the government's application of its statutory, regulatory, and taxing powers to pursue them, as a miscomprehension of man's nature and an assault on the individual's inalienable rights and the civil society. Underlying Locke's view of man, society, and government is the individual's right to the value he creates with his own labor and in his own property (which may be physical and/or intellectual) now and in the future, for it is central to his nature and existence. The right of all individuals to try to acquire property, and once acquired to secure it, is a right that no man or government can legitimately deny him, and which just governments are instituted to preserve and protect. Although some will become wealthy and some will not—that is, the result will be unequal when comparing individual to individual—the poorest man can become rich and the richest man can become poor depending on how each applies his labor. Furthermore, the protection of private property applies not only to that which exists today, but to that which is earned in the future, thereby encouraging industriousness and the expansion of wealth in successive generations, to the good of the individual and society.

Moreover, whereas Marx and Engels later argued for the destruction of what they called the bourgeois, or the feudal lords and later capitalists, insisting there can otherwise be no justice for the laborer, Locke explained that the coercive redistribution of wealth through government's abuse of law and misapplication of rights destroys individual liberty; ambition, productivity, and wealth; and the purpose of the commonwealth. Instead, society and government should ensure that all individuals, regardless of their circumstances of birth, are unmolested in their inalienable rights. If all are free and secure in this regard, there can be no predestined or official class structure or caste system. In this sense, property rights are the great equalizer—not of outcomes but opportunity. This is the surest way to expand economic opportunity for the greatest number. Communism, and its socialist progeny, is tyranny. And it is tyranny without end since equality of economic outcomes is an illusion, requiring constant repression and plundering.

Locke summed up the purpose of government this way: "Absolute arbitrary power, can neither of them consist with the ends of society and government, which men would not quit the freedom of the state of nature for, and tie themselves up under, were it not to preserve their lives, liberties and fortunes, and by stated rules of right and property to secure their peace and quiet. . . . For all the power the government has, being only for the good of the society, as it ought not to be arbitrary and at pleasure, so it ought to be exercised by established and promulgated laws, and the rulers too, kept within their bounds. . . ." (11, 137)

Locke's extraordinary insight into the nature of man, the sovereignty of the individual, and the ideological threats that have and will menace the civil society by those who exercise governmental authority is much more than an academic undertaking. Few before Locke or since have had such a thorough grasp of the human condition and enormous influence on Western civilization.

CHAPTER SEVEN

THE INFLUENCE OF LOCKE ON THE FOUNDERS

IN 1776, THE CONTINENTAL Congress established the Committee of Five to draft a declaration to the world setting forth the American colonies' justification for seeking independence from Great Britain. It appointed John Adams of Massachusetts, Roger Sherman of Connecticut, Benjamin Franklin of Pennsylvania, Robert R. Livingston of New York,[1] and Thomas Jefferson of Virginia. The committee assigned Jefferson the task of drafting the original version. Jefferson's draft was modified by Franklin and Adams and submitted to Congress. Congress made further modifications. But the basic document remained largely unchanged from Jefferson's version.

For the purposes of this discussion, it is important to recognize the profound influence Locke's *Second Treatise* had on the Founders, especially Jefferson. The Declaration of Independence represents the most prominent, official, consensus position of the Founders' rationale for declaring independence and, importantly, the philosophical origin of the new country. Jefferson and the delegates borrowed heavily from Locke's thinking and words.

EXAMPLE 1

In the *Second Treatise* [2] Locke writes, "The constitution of the legislative is the first and fundamental act of society, whereby provision is made for the continuation of their union under the direction of persons and bonds of laws, made by persons authorized thereunto, but the consent and appointment of the people, without which no one man, or number of men, amongst them can have authority of making laws that shall be binding to the rest. When anyone, or more, shall take upon them to make laws, whom the people have not appointed so to do, they make laws without authority, which the people are not therefore bound to obey; by which means they come again to be out of subjection, and may constitute to themselves a new legislative, as they think best, being in full liberty to resist the force of those, who without authority would impose any thing upon them" (19, 212).

Locke's asserting that laws made by men or governments without the consent of the governed are illegitimate and no man is bound to them. Under these circumstances, men are not only free to resist such a force, but they are free to form a new government.

Locke also writes, "[W]henever the legislators endeavour to take away and destroy the property of the people, or to reduce them to slavery under arbitrary power, they put themselves into a state of war with the people, who are thereupon absolved from any farther obedience, and are left to the common refuge which God hath provided for all men against force and violence. . . . What I have said . . . concerning the legislative in general holds true concerning the supreme executor, who having a double trust put in him, both to have a part in the legislative and the supreme execution of the law, acts against both, when he goes about to set up his own arbitrary will as the law of the society" (19, 222).

Locke is not only underscoring his earlier point about man's right to resist the illegitimate, arbitrary power of government, particularly relating to his property rights; he is going further—that is, no government, including one established by the consent of the governed, has authority to violate man's inalienable rights.

Locke explains that the law of nature exists above all else, and all men are required to obey it, including those who hold public office. "Thus the law of Nature stands as an eternal rule to all men, legislators as well as others. The rules that they make for other men's actions, must, as well as their own and other men's actions, be conformable to the law of Nature, i.e., to the will of God, of which that is a declaration, and the fundamental law of nature being the preservation of mankind, no human sanction can be good, or valid against it" (11, 135).

The first sentence of the Declaration encapsulates Locke's view of the preeminence of natural law and the right to disobey and, indeed, throw off a government that abuses its power. It states, "When in the Course of human events, it becomes necessary for one people to dissolve the political bands which have connected them with another, and to assume among the powers of the earth, the separate and equal station to which the Laws of Nature and of Nature's God entitle them, a decent respect to the opinions of mankind requires that they should declare the causes which impel them to the separation."

EXAMPLE 2

Locke writes, "The state of Nature has a law of Nature to govern it, which obliges everyone, and reason, which is that law, teaches all mankind who will but consult it, that being all equal and in-dependent, no one ought to harm another in his life, health, liberty or possessions, for men being all the workmanship of one omnipotent and infinitely wise Maker; all the servants of one sovereign Master, sent into the world by His order and about His business. . . . And, being furnished with like faculties, sharing all in one community of Nature, there cannot be supposed any such subordination among us that may authorize us to destroy one an-other, as if we were made for one another's uses, as the inferior ranks of creatures are for ours. Everyone as he is bound to preserve himself, and not to quit his station willfully, so by the like reason, when his own preservation comes not in competition, ought he as much as he can to preserve the rest of mankind, and not unless it be to do justice on an offender, take away or impair the life, or what tends to the preservation of the life, the liberty, health, limb, or goods of another" (2, 6).

The Founders embraced Locke's vision that all men are blessed by God with inalienable rights—"the life, the liberty, health, limb, or goods of another"—which they described this way: "We hold these truths to be self-evident, that all men are created equal, that they are endowed by their Creator with certain unalienable rights, that among these are life, liberty and the pursuit of happiness." It is the job of government to preserve those rights.

EXAMPLE 3

Again, Locke explains that any government not established by the consent of the governed is illegitimate and, therefore, its laws are illegitimate. "Nor can any edict of anybody else, in what form soever conceived, or by what power soever backed, have the force and obligation of a law which has not its sanction from that legis- lative which the public has chosen and appointed; for without this the law could not have that which is absolutely necessary to its be- ing a law, the consent of the society, over whom nobody can have a power to make laws but by their own consent and by authority received from them. . . ." (11, 134)

Nor can a government established by the consent of the people exercise absolute power or surrender its legitimate power to an- other. In either case, the people are free to replace the officials with others or disband the government altogether and form a new one. "Whensoever, therefore, the legislative shall . . . endeavor to grasp themselves, or put into the hands of any other, an absolute power over the lives, liberties, and estates of the people, by this breach of trust they forfeit the power the people had put into their hands for quite contrary ends, and it devolves to the people, who have a right to resume their original liberty, and by the establishment of a new legislative (such as they think fit) provide for their own safety and security, which is the end for which they are in society" (19, 222). "In these, and the like cases, when the government is dissolved, the people are at liberty to provide for themselves by erecting a new legislative differing from the other by the change of persons, or form, or both as they shall find it most for their safety and good" (19, 220).

The Founders agreed. They proclaimed in the Declaration, "That to secure these rights, governments are instituted among men, deriving their just powers from the consent of the governed. That whenever any form of government becomes destructive to these ends, it is the right of the people to alter or to abolish it, and to institute new government, laying its foundation on such principles and organizing its powers in such form, as to them shall seem most likely to effect their safety and happiness."

EXAMPLE 4

There should be no mistaking Locke's position with that of an anarchist. "[S]uch revolutions happen not upon every little mismanagement in public affairs. Great mistakes in the ruling part, many wrong and inconvenient laws, and all the slips of human frailty will be borne by the people without mutiny or murmur" (19, 225). Besides, he observes that "the people, who are more disposed to suffer than right themselves by resistance, are not apt to stir. People are not so easily got out of their old forms, as some are apt to suggest. They are hardly to be prevailed with to amend the acknowledged faults in the frame they have been accustomed to" (19, 223).

However, if the people are pushed too far by a tyrannical government, revolution is not only legitimate but possible. "But if a long train of abuses, prevarications, and artifices, all tending the same way, make the design visible to the people, it is not to be wondered that they should then rouse themselves, and endeavour to put the rule into such hands which may secure to them the ends for which government was at first erected. . . ." (19, 225)

The Declaration not only captures the essence of Locke's point in this regard, but it borrows certain of his phrases and words. "Prudence, indeed, will dictate that Governments long established should not be changed for light and transient causes; and accordingly all experience hath shewn, that mankind are more disposed to suffer, while evils are sufferable, than to right themselves by abolishing the forms to which they are accustomed. But when a long train of abuses and usurpations, pursuing invariably the same Object evinces a design to reduce them under absolute Despotism, it is their right, it is their duty, to throw off such Government, and to provide new Guards for their future security."

EXAMPLE 5

Having set forth the philosophical foundation for the new nation in the Declaration, much of what remains of the proclamation is a bill of particulars—the "long train of abuses"—indicting the king for his tyrannical acts and justifying the dissolution of his rule and the advent of revolution. "The history of the present King of

Great Britain is a history of repeated injuries and usurpations, all having in direct object the establishment of an absolute tyranny over these states. To prove this, let facts be submitted to a candid world." Hence, in this the Founders, and Jefferson specifically, once again turn to Locke for guidance when reciting the twenty-seven allegations against George III.

In the Declaration's first ten charges, the king is accused of refusing to accept the laws of the colonies, interfering with the operations of the colonies, supplanting colonial law with his own dictates, and dissolving representative legislatures—that is, an obvious plan of subjugation against the colonists by means of usurpation, abuse, obstruction, and neglect. Indeed, under the Declaration's sixth charge, the Founders assert that whatever authority the king once had over the colonies has already been dissolved. "[T]he legislative powers . . . have returned to the people at large for their exercise. . . ." By Locke's standards, the charges provided more than enough evidence of tyranny and validation for revolution. The remaining seventeen charges accuse the king of waging war against the colonies, making his own government illegitimate and allegiance to it self-defeating. After all, men adhere to governments that have as their purpose the preservation and protection of their inalienable rights.

EXAMPLE 6

Locke's writings also include emphatic condemnations of slavery. Slavery conflicted with Locke's view of liberty, rights, labor, and property. In the first sentence of the first chapter of the *First*

Treatise of Government, Locke writes bluntly, "Slavery is so vile and miserable an Estate of Man, and so directly opposite to the generous Temper and Courage of our Nation; that 'tis hardly to be conceived, that an *Englishman,* much less *Gentleman,* should plead for't" (1, 1).

In the *Second Treatise,* Locke elaborates on slavery's perniciousness. "Though the earth and all inferior creatures be common to all men, yet every man has a 'property' in his own 'person.' This nobody has any right to but himself. The 'labor' of his body and the 'work' of his hands, we may say, are properly his. Whatsoever, then, he removes out of the state that Nature hath provided and left it in, he hath mixed his labor with, and joined to it something that is his own, and thereby makes it his property. It being by him removed from the common state makes it his property. It being by him removed from the common state Nature placed it in, it hath by his labor something annexed to it that excludes the common right of other men. For this 'labor' being the unquestionable property of the laborer, no man but he can have a right to what that is once joined to, at least where there is enough, and as good left in common for others" (5, 16).

Locke also observed, "The Natural liberty of man is to be free from any superior power on earth, and not to be under the will or legislative authority of man, but to have only the law of Nature for his rule. The liberty of man in society is to be under no legislative power but that established by consent in the commonwealth, nor under the domination of any will, restraint of any law, but what that legislative shall enact according to the trust put in it. . . . [F]reedom of men under government is to have a standing rule to live by, common to everyone of that society, and made by the legislative power erected in it. A liberty to follow my own will in all things where the rule prescribes not, not to be subject to the inconstant, uncertain, unknown, arbitrary will of another man, as freedom of nature is to be under no other restraint by the law of Nature" (4, 21). "For a man, not having the power of his own life, cannot by compact or his own consent enslave himself to anyone, nor put himself under the absolute, arbitrary power of another to take away his life when he pleases. Nobody can give more power than he has himself, and he that cannot take away his own life cannot give that power over it" (4, 22).

Although Jefferson was a slaveholder, his original draft of the Declaration included a charge against the king for his promotion of slavery, which was removed by Congress in the Declaration's final version because of objections by members from Georgia and South Carolina. However, Jefferson's original version provided that "he [the king] has waged cruel war against human nature itself, violating its most sacred rights of life & liberty in the persons of a distant people who never offended him, captivating & carrying them into slavery in another hemisphere, or to incur miserable death in their transportation thither. This piratical warfare, the opprobrium of *infidel* powers, is the warfare of the CHRISTIAN king of Great Britain. Determined to keep open a market where MEN should be bought & sold, he has prostituted his negative for suppressing every legislative attempt to prohibit or to restrain this execrable commerce . . ."[3]

Even with the deletion of the antislavery charge, Jefferson and many of those signing the Declaration were setting in motion a course of events that would eventually challenge the legitimacy of slavery. After all, it was not possible to establish a nation based on inalienable rights—acknowledging every man's sovereignty and equal right to the fruits of his own labor as a law of nature and thus God's law—yet thereafter sanction slavery. And each of the original colonies gave allegiance to the Declaration, without exception. The idea and principle of the inseparability of liberty and property were at the core of America's origin.

Locke's impact on another important founder, George Mason, is evident in Mason's original draft of the Virginia Declaration of Rights, which was written between May 20 and 26, 1776, and preceded by several weeks the adoption of the Declaration of Independence. Mason would later become a delegate from Virginia to the Constitutional Convention and ultimately refused to sign the Constitution, for he insisted on the inclusion of a bill of rights. (Of course, a bill of rights was later adopted.) Mason was a slaveholder, but he argued, among other things, that the Constitution did not do enough to prohibit the slave trade and the spread of slavery.

The similarities between Mason's draft of the Virginia Declaration of Rights and the subsequent Declaration of Independence are obvious. And, again, Locke's influence is visible throughout the document. Mason wrote, "That all Men are born equally free and independent, and have certain inherent natural Rights, of which they can not by any Compact, deprive or divest their Posterity; among which are the Enjoyment of Life and Liberty, with the Means of acquiring and possessing Property, and pursuing and obtaining Happiness and Safety. That Power is, by God and Nature, vested in, and consequently derived from the People. . . ." Mason shares Locke's view of God-given, immutable natural rights, which all men are vested with at birth, and which government has neither the power to grant nor deny.

The draft included, "That Government is, or ought to be, instituted for the common Benefit, Protection, and Security of the People, Nation, or Community; of all the various Modes and Forms of Government, that is best, which is capable of producing the greatest Degree of Happiness and Safety, and is most effectually secured against the Danger of mal-administration. And that whenever any Government shall be found inadequate, or contrary to these Purposes, a Majority of the Community had an indubitable, inalienable, and indefeasible Right to reform, alter or abolish it, in such Manner as shall be judged most conducive to the Public Weal." Consistent with Locke's view, if the government ceases to nurture, preserve, and protect man's inalienable rights, the people are free if not obligated to alter it.

Furthermore, Mason wrote that government cannot simply seize someone's property. Nor are the people required to comply with laws imposed by a government established without their consent. "That no part of a Man's Property can be taken from him, or applied to public uses, without the Consent of himself, or his legal Representatives; nor are the People bound by any Laws, but such as they have in like Manner assented to for their common Good." Again, this is a Lockean formulation.

Mason also insisted on impartial justice. "That in all controversies respecting Property, and in Suits between Man and Man, the ancient Trial by Jury is preferable to any other, and ought to be held sacred." This is a main justification Locke provides for men to leave the state of nature and join a commonwealth. Locke wrote, "And thus all private judgment of every particular member being excluded, the community comes to be umpire, and by understanding indifferent rules and men authorized by the community for their execution, decides all the differences that may happen between any members of that society concerning any matter of right, and punishes those offenses which any member hath committed against the society with such penalties as the law has established. . . ." (7, 87)

It is also noteworthy that James Madison—a close Jefferson ally who later worked with Jefferson to create the Democratic-Republican Party, served as Jefferson's secretary of state, replaced Jefferson as rector of the University of Virginia, and is considered by most the Father of the Constitution—was also significantly influenced by Locke, as were others.

Explaining why men transition from the state of nature to the commonwealth, Locke observed, as he did repeatedly in the *Second Treatise*, that liberty, labor, and property are part of a whole. He wrote that "it is not without reason that [man] seeks out and is willing to join in society with others who are already united, or have a mind to unite for the mutual preservation of their lives, liberties and estates, which I call by the general name—property" (9, 123). Furthermore, "the great and chief end . . . of men uniting into commonwealths, and putting themselves under government, is the preservation of their property. . . ." (9, 124) Locke also explained that there is inevitably an unequal distribution of property resulting from the manner in which a man applies his labor. "As much land as a man tills, plants, improves, cultivates, and can use the product of, so much is his property. He by his labor does, as it were, enclose it from the common" (5, 31). "He gave it to the use of the industrious and rational (and labor was to be his title to it); not to the fancy or covetousness of the quarrelsome and contentious" (5, 33).

In *Federalist* 10, which is among the many essays comprising the *Federalist Papers*—the most prominent and brilliant advocacy for the Constitution's ratification—Madison wrote, "The diversity in the faculties of men from which the rights of property originate, is not less an insuperable obstacle to a uniformity of interests. The protection of these faculties is the first object of Government. . . ."

In 1792, writing in the *National Gazette*, Madison underscored his embrace of Locke's broad view of the mutual dependency of individual and property rights. Madison began his essay by arguing that the term property "means 'that dominion which one man claims and exercises over the external things of the world, in exclusion of every other individual.' "[4] Madison borrows nearly the exact wording from William Blackstone, the great eighteenth-century British legal scholar.[5] However, as Madison surely knew, and as is clear on the surface, Blackstone's words reflect Locke's concept of property rights.

Madison wrote further that property "in its larger and juster meaning . . . embraces every thing to which a man may attach a value and have a right; and *which leaves to every one else the like advantage*. In the former sense, a man's land, or merchandize, or money is called his property. In the latter sense, a man has a property in his opinions and the free communication of them. He has a property of peculiar value in his religious opinions, and in the profession and practice dictated by them. He has a property very dear to him in the safety and liberty of his person. He has an equal property in the free use of his faculties and free choice of the objects on which to employ them. In a word, as a man is said to have a right to his property, he may be equally said to have a property in his rights. . . . Government is instituted to protect property of every sort; as well that which lies in the various rights of individuals, as that which the term particularly expresses. This being the end of government, that alone is a *just* government, which *impartially* secures to every man, whatever is his *own*." Madison added, "That is not a just government, nor is property secure under it, where the property which a man has in his personal safety and personal liberty, is violated by arbitrary seizures of one class of citizens for the service of the rest. . . . That is not a just government, nor is property secure under it, where arbitrary restrictions, exemptions, and monopolies deny to part of its citizens the free use of their faculties, and free choice of their occupations, which not only constitute their property in the general sense of the word; but are the means of acquiring property strictly so called. . . ."[6]

Madison also drafted the first version of the Takings Clause of what became the Fifth Amendment to the Constitution, guaranteeing the legal protection of real property from confiscation by the federal government without lawful justification and compensation. He wrote that a person could not "be . . . obliged to relinquish his property, where it may be necessary for public use, without just compensation."[7] The final version, of course, reads that "private property shall [not] be taken for public use without just compensation."[8]

Locke's writings were not the only philosophical and political influences in the colonies. For example, especially Charles de Montesquieu, as well as several eighteenth-century thinkers who together make up the Enlightenment, played a significant role. However, Locke was the most prominent during the revolutionary period. Professor Bernard Bailyn, having conducted an extensive examination of the period's pamphlets—which were among the most important manner of communication at the time—observed, "In pamphlet after pamphlet the American writers cited Locke on natural rights and on the social and governmental contract. . . ."[9]

So important was Locke to the founding that it is difficult to imagine what kind of nation, if any, the Founders would have established had Locke not lived. The Founders were enlightened and well-educated men who embraced science, reason, experience, tradition, and knowledge. They were men of faith who preached tolerance, morality, and virtue. They used all these qualities and values to draw upon their collective wisdom in organizing the nation around the principles of natural law and natural rights. As such, they appropriated and ratified philosophical arguments espoused by Locke, thereby amalgamating the philosophical with the political. They committed themselves in the founding document, in revolution, and in governance to a respect for human dignity and life through the enshrinement of inalienable individual rights and liberties; to free enterprise and private property rights, where the industrious not only enhance their own lives but contribute to the overall well-being of society; to a representative government of divided authority and limited powers directed at preserving and protecting the individual's inalienable rights and liberties; and to a just law applied impartially to all individuals.

Looked at another way, the utopian models of Plato's *Republic*, More's *Utopia*, Hobbes's *Leviathan*, and Marx's *Communist Manifesto* could not be more repugnant to America's philosophical and political foundation. Each of the utopias, in their own way, are models for totalitarian regimes managed by masterminds who rule over men as subjects. The individual exists to serve the state, to be reshaped and molded by the state, and the state exists to serve the masterminds' cause. There are no inalienable rights, only those liberties and rights conferred on men by the state, should the state decide to confer them at all. The individual's labor and property belong to the state or are controlled by the state, which determines how best to allocate them, thereby enslaving the individual to the state. There is no impartial law or impartial adjudication of the law, only rule by torment and, if necessary, iron fist to ensure compliance with utopian faith. There is no tolerance for individual self-interest or even self-preservation, for equality in terms of conformity and outcomes is paramount.

Whereas the utopians start from the premise that the individual must be managed and suppressed by masterminds for the greater good, Locke opposed authoritarianism and sought to uncover the true nature of man and the environment most conducive to his fulfillment and happiness. Having experienced the wrath of monarchy, in Locke the Founders discovered a patron saint.

CHAPTER EIGHT

CHARLES DE MONTESQUIEU AND
REPUBLICAN GOVERNMENT

JUST AS JOHN LOCKE'S influence on the Founders and the Declaration of Independence was profound, French philosopher Charles de Montesquieu, who lived from 1689 to 1755, was enormously important to the Framers of the Constitution, particularly respecting the form of government and separation of powers. However, in his seminal and extensive work, *The Spirit of the Laws*, Montesquieu also wrote at length about the nature of man and societies.

Montesquieu explains that "[p]rior to all these laws are the laws of nature, so named because they derive uniquely from the constitution of our being. To know them well, one must consider a man before the establishment of societies. The laws he would receive in such a state will be the laws of nature. The law that impresses on us the idea of a creator and thereby leads us toward him is the first of the *natural laws* in importance, though not first in the order of these laws. A man in the state of nature would have the faculty of knowing rather than knowledge. It is clear that his first ideas would not be speculative ones; he would think of the preservation of his being before seeking the origin of his being. Such a man would at first feel only his weakness; his timidity would be extreme. . . . In this state, each feels himself inferior; he scarcely feels himself an equal. Such men would not seek to attack one another, and peace would be the first natural law."[1]

Like Locke, Montesquieu rejects explicitly Thomas Hobbes's view of the state of man in nature. He observes that "Hobbes gives men first the desire to subjugate one another, but this is not reasonable. The idea of empire and domination is so complex and depends on so many other ideas, that it would not be the one they would first have. Hobbes asks, *If men are not naturally in a state of war, why do they always carry arms and why do they have keys to lock their doors?* But one feels that what can happen to men only after the establishment of societies, which induced them to find motives for attacking others and for defending themselves, is attributed to them before the establishment. . . . I have said that fear would lead men to flee one another, but the marks of mutual fear would soon persuade them to approach one another" (1, 1, 2).

As men join together in society and subsequently form governments, Montesquieu argues, the state of war begins. By this he means that nations need to protect themselves from other nations, and people within each nation must protect themselves from each other and from a government. There can be no political liberty without law. Respecting the establishment of laws, Montesquieu explains "Considered as living in a society that must be maintained, they have laws concerning the relation between those who govern and those who are governed, and this is the POLITICAL RIGHT. Further, they have laws concerning the relation that all citizens have with one another, and this is the CIVIL RIGHT" (1, 1, 2).

Montesquieu wrote of the nature of governments. "There are three kinds of government: REPUBLICAN, MONARCHICAL, and DESPOTIC. To discover the nature of each, the idea of them held by the least educated of men is sufficient. I assume three definitions, or rather, three facts: one, *republican government is that in which the people as a body, or only a part of the people, have sovereign power; monarchical government is that in which one alone governs, but by fixed and established laws; whereas, in despotic government, one alone, without law and without rule, draws everything along by his will and caprices*" (1, 1, 2). In republican government, Montesquieu explains, the people must be able to vote in elections. "A people having sovereign power should do for itself all it can do well, and what it cannot do well, it must do through ministers. Ministers do not belong to the people unless the people name them; therefore it is a fundamental maxim of this government that the people should name their ministers, that is, their magistrates" (1, 2, 1).

Montesquieu points out, "There is this difference between the nature of the government and its principle: its nature is that which makes it what it is, and its principle, that which makes it act. The one is its particular structure, and the other is the human passions that set it in motion" (1, 3, 1). He explains, "There need not be much integrity for a monarchical or despotic government to maintain or sustain itself. The force of the law in the one and the prince's ever-raised arm in the other can rule or contain the whole." As for republican government, Montesquieu asserts that "in a popular state there must be an additional spring, which is VIRTUE. What I say is confirmed by the entire body of history and is quite in conformity with the nature of things. For it is clear that less virtue is needed in a monarchy, where the one who sees to the execution of the laws judges himself above the laws, than in a popular government, where the one who sees to the execution of the laws feels that he is subject to them himself and that he will bear their weight. . . . But in a popular government when the laws have ceased to be executed, as this can come only from the corruption of the republic, the state is already lost" (1, 3, 3). In despotic government, "virtue is not at all necessary to it. . . ." (1, 3, 8)

Montesquieu saw despotism, including its frequent antecedent, anarchy, as a continuing threat to republican government. "When that virtue ceases, ambition enters those hearts that can admit it, and avarice enters them all. Desires change their objects: that which one used to love, one loves no longer. One was free under the laws, one wants to be free against them. Each citizen is like a slave who has escaped from his master's house. What was a *maxim* is now called *severity*; what was a *rule* is now called *constraint*; what was *vigilance* is now called *fear*. There, frugality, not the desire to possess, is avarice. Formerly the goods of individuals made up the public treasury; the public treasury has now become the patrimony of individuals. The republic is a cast-off husk, and its strength is no more than the power of a few citizens and the license of all" (1, 3, 3).

Montesquieu warned, "In despotic states the nature of the

government requires extreme obedience, and the prince's will, once known, should produce its effect as infallibly as does one ball thrown against another. No tempering, modification, accommodation, terms, alternatives, negotiations, remonstrances, nothing as good or better can be proposed. Man is a creature that obeys a creature that wants. He can no more express his fears about a future event than he can blame his lack of success on the caprice of fortune. There, men's portion, like beasts', is instinct, obedience, and chastisement. It is useless to counter with natural feelings, respect for a father, tenderness for one's children and women, laws of honor, or the state of one's health; one has received the order and that is enough" (1, 3, 10). Yet, despite man's preference for liberty, most live under tyranny. Montesquieu explained that "despite men's love of liberty, despite their hatred of violence, most peoples are subjected to this type of government. This is easy to understand. In order to form a moderate government, one must combine powers, regulate them, temper them, make them act; one must give one power a ballast, so to speak, to put it in a position to resist another; this is a masterpiece of legislation that chance rarely produces and prudence is rarely allowed to produce. By contrast, a despotic government leaps to view, so to speak; it is uniform throughout; as only passions are needed to establish it, everyone is good enough for that" (1, 5, 14).

It follows that virtue is mostly impossible in a monarchy and nonexistent under despotism, but is crucial to sustain a republican government. "Virtue, in a republic, is a very simple thing: it is love of the republic; it is a feeling and not a result of knowledge; the lowest man in the state, like the first, can have this feeling." However, virtue alone is not enough. "Despotic government has fear as its principle; and not many laws are needed for timid, ignorant, beaten-down people" (1, 5, 13), but republican government requires fixed, established laws adopted by the representatives of the people, which create a culture of support for the republic. "Laws must relate to the nature and the principle of the government that is established or that one wants to establish, whether those laws form it as do political laws, or maintain it, as do civil laws" (1, 1, 3).

Montesquieu warns of the tyranny of concentrated power resulting from either unjust laws or the application of laws unjustly, and the anarchy of radical egalitarianism that leads to despotism. He wrote, "The principle of democracy is corrupted not only when the spirit of equality is lost but also when the spirit of extreme equality is taken up and each one wants to be the equal of those chosen to command. So the people, finding intolerable even the power they entrust to the others, want to do everything themselves: to deliberate for the senate, to execute for the magistrates, and to cast aside all judges" (1, 8, 2). As a result, Montesquieu observed, "democracy has to avoid two excesses: the spirit of inequality, which leads it to aristocracy or to the government of one alone, and the spirit of extreme equality, which leads it to the despotism of one alone, as the despotism of one alone ends by conquest" (1, 8, 2).

Montesquieu also fears the destructive consequences of excessive taxation on liberty. He wrote, "These great advantages of liberty have caused the abuse of liberty itself. Because moderate government has produced remarkable results, this moderation has been abandoned; because large taxes have been raised, one has wanted to raise excessive ones; and, disregarding the hand of liberty that gave this present, one has turned to servitude, which refuses everything. Liberty has produced excessive taxes, but the effect of these excessive taxes is to produce servitude in their turn, and the effect of servitude is to produce a decrease in taxes" (2, 13, 15). Montesquieu argued that in "moderate states" the outright confiscation of property is destructive of the individual. "Confiscations would render the ownership of goods uncertain; they would despoil innocent children; they would destroy a family man when it was only a question of punishing a guilty man. In republics, confiscations would have the ill effect of taking away the equality which is their soul, by depriving a citizen of his physical necessities" (1, 5, 15). Montesquieu considered excessive taxation and the confiscation of private property an assault on equality— that is, the individual's liberty and rights. Montesquieu's view of equality, therefore, is consistent with Locke's.

Montesquieu also viewed commerce as essential to the character of republican government. "[T]he spirit of commerce brings with it the spirit of frugality, economy, moderation, work, wisdom, tranquility, order, and rule. . . ." (1, 5, 6) Furthermore, commerce helps promote republican mores in other countries. "Commerce cures destructive prejudices, and it is an almost general rule that everywhere there are gentle mores, there is commerce and that everywhere there is commerce, there are gentle mores. . . ." (4, 20, 1) Commerce also encourages prosperity. "In short, one's belief that one's prosperity is more certain in these states makes one undertake everything, and because one believes that what one has acquired is secure, one dares to expose it in order to acquire more; only the means for acquisition are at risk; now, men expect much of their fortune. . . ." Conversely, despotism begets hardship and poverty. "As for the despotic state, it is useless to talk about it. General rule: in a nation that is in servitude, one works more to preserve than to acquire; in a free nation, one works more to acquire than to preserve" (4, 20, 4).

Montesquieu explained that unlike the poor in republican governments, who in freedom can better their circumstances, in despotic states the poor have no hope. "There are two sorts of poor peoples: some are made so by the harshness of the government, and these people are capable of almost no virtue because their poverty is a part of their servitude; the others are poor only because they have disdained or because they did not know the comforts of life, and these last can do great things because this poverty is a part of their liberty" (4, 20, 3).

Industrious men and societies are also to be encouraged. "Countries which have been made inhabitable by the industry of men and which need that same industry in order to exist call for moderate government" (3, 18, 6). "Men, by their care and their good laws, have made the earth more fit to be their home. We see rivers flowing where there were lakes and marshes; it is a good that nature did not make, but which is maintained by nature. When the Persians were the masters of Asia, they permitted those who diverted the water from its source to a place that had not yet been watered to enjoy it for five generations, and, as many streams flow from the Taurus mountains, they spared no expense in getting water from there. Today, one finds it in one's fields and gardens without knowing where it comes from. Thus, just as destructive nations do evil things that last longer than themselves, there are industrious nations that do good things that do not end with themselves" (3, 18, 7). Montesquieu, like Locke, explained that commerce, industriousness, and laws that inspire them require a moderate or republican government, which, in combination, preserve and improve the society. Alternatively, "Every lazy nation is grave; for those who do not work regard themselves as sovereigns of those who work" (3, 19, 9).

Moreover, commerce is a natural outgrowth of republican government, where individuals are largely free to make self-interested economic decisions. Montesquieu wrote, "Commerce is related to the constitution. In government by one alone, it is ordinarily founded on luxury, and though it is also founded on real needs, its principal object is to procure for the nation engaging in it all that serves its arrogance, its delights, and its fancies. In government by many, it is more often founded on economy. Traders, eyeing all the nations of earth, take to one what they bring from another. . . ." (4, 20, 4)

Montesquieu, always mindful of history's preference for tyranny, argued that political liberty exists within the context of a constitution—a fixed, established law. The constitution must institute a governing structure that controls the governors. He proposed that the three powers of government—that is, the legislative, the executive, and the judicial—be divided into three separate entities. In this not only does Montesquieu add significant clarity to Locke's notion of division of powers, but his words have a major influence on the future constitution of the American republic, as they did in the state constitutions.

Montesquieu wrote, "Political liberty in a citizen is that tranquility of spirit which comes from the opinion each one has of his security, and in order for him to have this liberty the government must be such that one citizen cannot fear another citizen. When legislative power is united with executive power in a single person or in a simple body of magistracy, there is no liberty, because one can fear that the same monarch or senate that makes tyrannical laws will execute them tyrannically. Nor is there liberty if the power of judging is not separate from legislative power and from executive power. If it were joined to legislative power, the power over the life and liberty of the citizens would be arbitrary, for the judge would be the legislator. If it were joined to executive power, the judge could have the force of an oppressor. All would be lost if the same man or the same body of principal men, either of nobles, or of the people, exercised these three powers: that of making the laws, that of executing public resolutions, and that of judging the crimes or the disputes of individuals" (2, 2, 6).

Montesquieu urged an independent and temporary judiciary in which judges, chosen from the people, strictly adhered to the law. He wrote, "The power of judging should not be given to a permanent senate but should be exercised by persons drawn from the body of the people at certain times of the year in the manner prescribed by law to form a tribunal which lasts only as long as necessity requires. . . . But though tribunals should not be fixed, judgments should be fixed to such a degree that they are never anything but a precise text of the law. If judgments were the individual opinion of a judge, one would live in this society without knowing precisely what engagements one has contracted" (2, 2, 6). Therefore, Montesquieu insisted that the role of a judge is to apply the law, not impose his opinion or prejudice. The latter approach is destructive of the nature of the judiciary and the broader republican government.

Furthermore, in regard to governing, Montesquieu raised numerous cautions to legislators, which, if ignored, he believed could gradually lead to despotism.

• The government should not force a way upon the people against their will, for to do so is tyranny by legislation. "There are two sorts of tyranny: a real one, which consists in the violence of the government, and one of opinion, which is felt when those who govern establish things that run counter to a nation's way of thinking" (3, 19, 3).

• It is essential, therefore, that in republican government, representatives avoid efforts intended to change the general spirit of the nation—that is, the legislator must help preserve and protect society, not eradicate it. As if describing the American people, Montesquieu wrote, "If there were in the world a nation which had a sociable humor, an openness of heart, a joy of life, a taste, an ease in communicating its thoughts; which was lively, pleasant, playful, sometimes imprudent, often indiscreet; and which had with all that, courage, generosity, frankness, and a certain point of honor, one should avoid disturbing its manners by laws, in order not to disturb its virtues. If the character is generally good, what difference do a few faults make? . . . The legislator is to follow the spirit of the nation when doing so is not contrary to the principles of the government, for we do nothing better than what we do freely and by following our natural genius. If one gives a pedantic spirit to a nation naturally full of gaiety, the state will gain nothing, either at home or abroad. Let it do frivolous things seriously and serious things gaily" (3, 19, 5).

• If change is considered desirable, the manner in which it is accomplished is, first and foremost, through persuasion, not legal coercion and government fiat. "We have said that the laws were the particular and precise institutions of the legislator and the mores and manners, the institutions of the nation in general. From this it follows that when one wants to change the mores and manners, one must not change them by laws, as this would appear to be too tyrannical; it would be better to change them by other mores and other manners" (3, 19, 9).

• Montesquieu argues that government should not attempt to correct or control all things and intervene in all matters. Government should be limited in its power, scope, and purposes. "May we be left as we are, said a gentleman of [a republican government]. Nature repairs everything. It has given us a vivacity capable of offending and one apt to make inconsiderate; this same vivacity is corrected by the politeness it brings us, by inspiring us with a taste for the world. . . . May we be left as we are. Our discretions joined to our harmlessness make unsuitable such laws as would curb our social humor" (3, 19, 6).

• Laws should reflect the uniqueness of societies. "[Laws] should be related to the *physical aspect* of the country; to the climate, be it freezing, torrid, or temperate; to the properties of the terrain, its location and extent; to the way of life of the peoples, be they plowmen, hunters, or herdsmen; they should relate to the degree of liberty that the constitution can sustain, to the religion of the inhabitants, their inclinations, their wealth, their number, their commerce, their mores, and their manners; finally, the laws are related to one another, to their origin, to the purpose of the legislator, and to the order of things on which they are established. They must be considered from all these points of view" (1, 1, 3). Clearly, Montesquieu argued that foreign governmental systems and laws do not necessarily serve the best interests of other countries, and he would object to their application by American jurists to interpreting the U.S. Constitution.

Montesquieu's concern is with the imprudence, and worse, the danger of republican government attempting to transform the civil society—including superseding the effects of religion, family, commerce, traditions, customs, mores, etc.—through legal coercion. In a chapter titled "How some legislators have confused principles that govern men," he wrote, "Mores and manners are usages that laws have not established, or that they have not been able, or have not wanted, to establish. The difference between laws and mores is that, while laws regulate the actions of the citizen, mores regulate the actions of the man. The difference between mores and manners is that the first are more concerned with internal, and the latter external, conduct" (3, 19, 16).

Montesquieu also believed that republican government does not work well over large regions, for the people are too diverse, their interests are too dissimilar, and their connection with the government is too distant. "It is in the nature of a republic to have only a small territory; otherwise, it can scarcely continue to exist. In a large republic, there are large fortunes, and consequently little moderation in spirits: the depositories are too large to put in the hands of a citizen; interests become particularized; at first a man feels he can be happy, great, and glorious without his homeland; and soon, that he can be great only on the ruins of his homeland. In a large republic, the common good is sacrificed to a thousand considerations; it is subordinated to exceptions, it depends upon accidents. In a small one, the public good is better felt, better known, lies nearer to each citizen; abuses are less extensive there and consequently less protected" (1, 8, 16). The issue of geographic size and diversity would become a major point of contention between the Federalists and Anti-Federalists during the ratification debates over the Constitution.

Furthermore, Montesquieu argued that a republic has the best chance of surviving if it consists of states that are also republican in nature. He wrote that "the federal constitution [a confederate government] should be composed of states of the same nature, above all republican states" (2, 9, 2). He recognized further that the states within a republic will be different in certain respects. "It is unlikely that the states that associate will be of the same size and have equal power. The republic of the Lycians was an association of twenty-three towns; the large ones had three votes in the common council; the medium-sized ones, two; the small ones, one. The republic of Holland is composed of seven provinces, large and small, each having one vote" (2, 9, 3). Of course, the United States Congress consists of two bodies—the House of Representatives, whose members are apportioned on the size of the population of each state, and the Senate, with two members from each state.

Obviously, Montesquieu's *The Spirit of the Laws* had virtually nothing in common with the utopias in Plato's *Republic*, More's *Utopia*, Hobbes's *Leviathan*, and, later, Marx's workers' paradise. Montesquieu's greatest concern was with despotism's threat to the individual and his political liberty. He argued for moderate, republican government, where the people choose their representatives and their representatives are prudent and virtuous. Aware of tyranny's resoluteness and the nature of political power, Montesquieu insisted that republics must separate the three powers of government into different branches to ensure they are not united under one person or centralized in one institution.

Furthermore, he emphasized that the law must be stable and predictable, reflective of society's mores, and made not to interfere with the individual's routine except in cases of actual necessity. When disputes arise or violations of law occur, they are to be adjudicated by individuals who are independent of the legislative and executive branches and adhere strictly to the law's meaning.

In addition to his separation-of-powers design, Montesquieu's warning about a republic's vulnerability should its size be too big and its scope too broad provided compelling political and intellectual justification for the federalism model in the American constitution. Even Montesquieu's discussion of the republic of the Lycians, where member towns (states) were allocated votes based on their size, and the republic of Holland, where member states were each allocated a single vote regardless of size, provided guidance for organizing America's future congress.

Montesquieu also rejected pure democracy, or extreme equality, where the public makes claims on the liberties and rights of the individual. He observed that property rights, commerce, and trade create wealth and economic progress, which benefit the individual and society. They also encourage peace between nations.

Montesquieu's view of man, man's nature, society, the law, and government would undoubtedly have led him to conclude that utopianism is despotism. He argued for liberty, equality properly understood, moderation, tolerance, and tradition. In political freedom, he believed the individual and society would prosper. Among his greatest thoughts were those aimed at the means of diminishing the opportunities for tyranny in government. Hence, Montesquieu's advocacy for republicanism, constitutionalism, justice, and the rule of law. In *The Spirit of the Laws*, Montesquieu would provide a road map for the American constitution, in which a system of government is established to represent a diverse and dynamic society, and the individual lives free from the cruelty and domination of others and the government itself.

CHAPTER NINE

THE INFLUENCE OF MONTESQUIEU
ON THE FRAMERS

THE TASK FACED BY the Framers of the Constitution was colossal. It made great sense that they would borrow from Charles de Montesquieu in developing a new government. He is believed to have been the most widely cited philosopher in America during the 1780s.[1]

It was certainly the case at the Constitutional Convention. Professor John R. Vile notes, "Delegates referred to Montesquieu a number of times during the Convention debates.[2] On June 1, Pennsylvania's James Wilson favorably cited Montesquieu's commendation of a confederated republic;[3] Montesquieu provided one of the authorities for Alexander Hamilton's speech to the Convention on June 18;[4] on June 23, Pierce Butler of South Carolina observed 'the great Montesquieu says, it is unwise to entrust persons with power, which by being abused operates to the advantage of those entrusted with it';[5] on June 30, Virginia's James Madison cited Montesquieu as authority for the view that the Lycian confederacy vested members with votes *proportional to their importance*;[6] on July 17 Madison cited Montesquieu as opposing undue dependence of the executive on the legislative body;[7] Maryland's James McHenry drew a similar conclusion on September 6;[8] on July 11, Virginia's Edmund Randolph cited Montesquieu as saying that suffrage is 'a fundamental article in Republican Govts.';[9] and other delegates reflected sentiments that Montesquieu had advocated."[10]

SEPARATION OF POWERS

Clearly, one of Montesquieu's most important contributions to the Constitution was his argument in *The Spirit of the Laws* for separate governing powers and against centralized, consolidated authority. Recall he wrote that "[w]hen legislative power is united with executive power in a single person or in a simple body of magistracy, there is no liberty, because one can fear that the same monarch or senate that makes tyrannical laws will execute them tyrannically. Nor is there liberty if the power of judging is not separate from legislative power and from executive power. If it were joined to legislative power, the power over the life and liberty of the citizens would be arbitrary, for the judge would be the legislator. If it were joined to executive power, the judge could have the force of an oppressor. All would be lost if the same man or the same body of principal men, either of nobles, or of the people, exercised these three powers: that of making the laws, that of executing public resolutions, and that of judging the crimes or the disputes of individuals" (2, 2, 6).

The delegates adopted this general design. The Constitution's first three articles set forth the division of power in the new federal government.

Article 1, Section 1 of the Constitution provides: "All legislative Powers herein granted shall be vested in a Congress of the United States, which shall consist of a Senate and House of Representatives."

Article 2, Section 1: "The executive Power shall be vested in a President of the United States of America. . . ."

Article 3, Section 1: "The judicial Power of the United States, shall be vested in one supreme Court, and in such inferior Courts as the Congress may from time to time ordain and establish. . . ."

Echoing Montesquieu, Madison explained later in *Federalist* 47 that "[t]he accumulation of all powers legislative, executive and judiciary in the same hands, whether of one, a few or many, and whether hereditary, self-appointed or elective, may justly be pronounced the very definition of tyranny. . . ." [11]

ENUMERATED POWERS

Even more, the delegates were not satisfied that dividing authority was enough to deter the despotism that might result from a central government. Therefore, rather than granting wide-ranging authority to each of the three branches to legislate, execute, and adjudicate, the delegates restricted the character of each branch by enumerating their specific powers for the purpose of protecting the liberty and rights of the individual, the sovereignty of the states, and the civil society.

The delegates' actions in limiting the role and scope of the federal branches also comports with Montesquieu's warnings about legislators in republican governments abusing their law-making power to destroy the nature of man and the civil society. Montesquieu cautioned, "There are two sorts of tyranny: a real one, which consists in the violence of the government, and one of opinion, which is felt when those who govern establish things that run counter to a nation's way of thinking" (3, 19, 3). "The legislator is to follow the spirit of the nation when doing so is not contrary to the principles of the government, for we do nothing better than what we do freely and by following our natural genius. . . ." (3, 19, 5) "[W]hen one wants to change the mores and manners [of a nation], one must not change them by laws, as this would appear to be too tyrannical; it would be better to change them by other mores and other manners" (3, 19, 9). "Nature repairs everything. . . . May we be left as we are. Our discretions joined to our harmlessness make unsuitable such laws as would curb our social humor" (3, 19, 6).

Nonetheless, the constitutional plan was attacked for not being clear enough about the separate roles of each of the three branches, one from the other. In defense, Madison wrote, "The oracle who is always consulted and cited on this subject, is the celebrated Montesquieu. If he be not the author of this invaluable precept in the science of politics, he has the merit at least of displaying, and recommending it most effectually to the attention of mankind. . . . [I]n saying 'there can be no liberty where the legislative and executive powers are united in the same person, or body of magistrates,' or 'if the power of judging be not separated from the legislative and executive powers,' he did not mean that these departments ought to have no *partial agency* in, or no *control* over the acts of each other. His meaning, as his own words import, and still more conclusively as illustrated by the example in his eye, can amount to no more than this, that where the *whole* power of one department is exercised by the same hands which possess the *whole* power of another department, the fundamental principles of a free constitution, are subverted. . . . If we look into the constitutions of the several states we find that notwithstanding the emphatical, and in some instance, the unqualified terms in which this axiom has been laid down, there is not a single instance in which the several departments of power have been kept absolutely separate and distinct."[12] Madison obviously rejected plenary power in a centralized government, and he believed that the Constitution averted it. However, he also argued that the delineation among the branches cannot be absolute.

FEDERALISM

Despite Madison's assurances, during the state ratification debates opponents of the Constitution (the Anti-Federalists) were not satisfied that, among other things, the states were protected from an overly powerful federal government. They argued that the conditions for despotism had not been sufficiently ameliorated by the enumeration of powers in distinct federal branches. Moreover, given the territorial expanse and diversity of the country, they insisted that the federal government would grow into a national government and suppress the states, making them impotent. Proponents of the Constitution (the Federalists) countered that the size and diversity of the country would ensure that the federal government was less able to empower itself beyond the authority granted it by the Constitution, and that state authority was, in fact, respected and protected. Thus, both sides insisted they were preserving state sovereignty, although they disagreed on the methods. There was consensus against an all-powerful or even overly powerful central government. Montesquieu was invoked repeatedly in the debate by the Federalists and Anti-Federalists.

In an important speech to the Pennsylvania Convention in support of the Constitution's ratification, James Wilson, among the most influential delegates to the Constitutional Convention, argued that the federal government would not become overbearing. He specifically addressed Montesquieu's caution.

"A very important difficulty arose from comparing the extent of the country to be governed with the kind of government which it would be proper to establish in it. It has been an opinion, countenanced by high authority [Montesquieu], 'that the natural property of small states is to be governed as a republic; of middling ones, to be subject to a monarch; and of large empires, to be swayed by a despotic prince; and that the consequence is that, in order to preserve the principles of the established government, the state must be supported in the extent it has acquired; and that the spirit of the state will alter in proportion as it extends or contracts its limits.' This opinion seems to be supported, rather than contradicted, by the history of the governments of the Old World. Here then the difficulty appeared in full view. . . . The idea of a confederate republic presented itself. This kind of constitution has been thought to have [as Montesquieu explained] 'all the internal advantages of a republican, together with the external force of a monarchical government.' Its description is, 'a convention, by which several states agree to become members of a larger one, which they intend to establish. It is a kind of assemblage of societies, that constitute a *new one*, capable of increasing by means of further association.' The *expanding* quality of such a government is peculiarly fitted for the United States, the greatest part of whose territory is yet uncultivated. Here then the difficulty appeared in full view. On one hand, the United States contain an immense extent of territory, and, according to the foregoing opinion, a despotic government is best adapted to that extent. On the other hand, it was well-known, that, however, the citizens of the United States might, with pleasure, submit to the legitimate restraints of a republican constitution, they would reject, with indignation, the fetters of despotism. . . ."[13]

Wilson discussed the various forms of government from which the delegates could construct the American system. He concluded, "The extent of territory, the diversity of climate and soil, the number, and greatness, and connection of lakes and rivers, with which the United States are intersected and almost surrounded, all indicate an enlarged government to be fit and advantageous for them. The principles and dispositions of their citizens indicate that in this government, liberty shall reign triumphant. Such indeed have been the general opinions and wishes entertained since the era of independence. If those opinions and wishes are as well-founded as they have been in general, the late Convention were justified in proposing to their constituents, one confederate republic as the best system of a national government for the United States." [14]

The Anti-Federalists at the Pennsylvania Convention responded, in part, by addressing Wilson's invocation of Montesquieu. "WE Dissent, first, because it is the opinion of the most celebrated writers on government, and confirmed by uniform experience, that a very extensive territory cannot be governed on the principles of freedom, otherwise than by a confederation of republics, possessing all the power of internal government; but united in the management of their general, and foreign concerns. If any doubt could have been entertained of the truth of the foregoing principle, it has been fully removed by the concession of Mr. [James] Wilson, one of the majority on this question, and who was one of the deputies in the late general convention. . . . [T]he powers vested in Congress by this constitution, must necessarily annihilate and absorb the legislative, executive, and judicial powers of the several states, and produce from their ruins one consolidated government, which from the nature of things will be *an iron-handed despotism*, as nothing short of the supremacy of despotic sway could connect and govern these United States under one government. . . ." [15]

The Anti-Federalists insisted that as configured under the Constitution, the states could not defend their sovereignty against a federal government fortified with such enormous power. "We apprehend that two coordinate sovereignties would be a solecism in politics. That therefore as there is no line of distinction drawn between the general, and state governments; as the sphere of their jurisdiction is undefined, it would be contrary to the nature of things, that both should exist together, one or the other would necessarily triumph in the fullness of dominion. However the contest could not be of long continuance, as the state governments are divested of every means of defense, and will be obliged by 'the supreme law of the land' *to yield at discretion.*"[16] The Anti-Federalists pointed out that explicit recognition of state authority provided in the Articles of Confederation was missing in the Constitution. "The new constitution, consistently with the plan of consolidation, contains no reservation of the rights and privileges of the state governments, which was made in the confederation of the year 1778, by article the 2nd. 'That each state retains its sovereignty, freedom, and independence, and every power, jurisdiction, and right, which is not by this confederation expressly delegated to the United States in Congress assembled.' "[17]

Sounding very much like Montesquieu, an Anti-Federalist writing under the alias Cato—and believed to be George Clinton of New York—noted, "The recital, or premises on which this new form of government is erected, declares a consolidation or union of all the thirteen parts, or states, into one great whole, under the form of the United States, for all the various and important purposes therein set forth.—But whoever seriously considers the immense extent of territory comprehended within the limits of the United States, together with the variety of its climates, productions, and commerce, the difference of extent, and number of inhabitants in all; the dissimilitude of interest, morals, and policies, in almost every one, will receive it as an intuitive truth, that a consolidated republican form of government therein, can never *form a perfect union, establish justice, insure domestic tranquility, promote the general welfare, and secure the blessings of liberty to you and your posterity*, for to these objects it must be directed: this unkindred legislature therefore, composed of interests opposite and dissimilar in their nature, will in its exercise, emphatically be, like a house divided against itself." [18]

Madison argued that the structure would work. In *Federalist* 45 he wrote, "The powers delegated by the proposed Constitution to the Federal Government are few and defined. Those which are to remain in the State Governments are numerous and indefinite. The former will be exercised principally on external objects, as war, peace, negotiation, and foreign commerce; with which last the power of taxation will for the most part be connected. The powers reserved to the several States will extend to all the objects, which, in the ordinary course of affairs, concern the lives, liberties, and properties of the people; and the internal order, improvement, and prosperity of the State." [19] In *Federalist* 39 Madison insisted that "the proposed government . . . extends to certain enumerated objects only, and leaves to the several States a residuary and inviolable sovereignty over all other objects. . . ." "[States and localities are] no more subject within their respective spheres to the general authority, than the general authority is subject to them, within its own sphere." [20] In *Federalist* 14, Madison observed, "It is to be remembered, that the general government is not to be charged with the whole power of making and administering laws. Its jurisdiction is limited to certain enumerated objects, which concern all the members of the republic, but which are not to be attained by the separate provisions of any. The subordinate governments which can extend their care to all those other objects, which can be separately provided for, will retain their due authority and activity." [21]

Moreover, in *Federalist* 9, Madison accused the Anti-Federalists of misconstruing Montesquieu. "The opponents of the PLAN proposed have, with great assiduity, cited and circulated the observations of Montesquieu on the necessity of a contracted territory for a republican government. But they seem not to have been apprised of the sentiments of that great man expressed in another part of his work, nor to have adverted to the consequences of the principle to which they subscribe with such ready acquiescence. When Montesquieu recommends a small extent for republics, the standards he had in view were of dimensions, far short of the limits of almost every one of these States. Neither Virginia, Massachusetts, Pennsylvania, New York, North Carolina, nor Georgia, can by any means be compared with the models, from which he reasoned and to which the terms of this description apply." Madison argues that if Montesquieu is read no further, "we shall be driven to the alternative, either of taking refuge at once in the arms of monarchy, or of splitting ourselves into an infinity of little jealous, clashing, tumultuous commonwealths, the wretched nurseries of unceasing discord and the miserable objects of universal pity or contempt. . . . So far are the suggestions of Montesquieu from standing in opposition to a general Union of the States, that he explicitly treats a CONFEDERATE REPUBLIC as the expedient for extending the sphere of popular government and reconciling the advantages of monarchy with those of republicanism." [22]

Madison then quoted directly from Montesquieu: "It is very probable . . . that mankind would have been obliged, at length, to live constantly under the government of a SINGLE PERSON, had they not contrived a kind of constitution, that has all the internal advantages of a republican, together with the external force of a monarchical government. I mean a CONFEDERATE REPUBLIC. This form of Government is a Convention, by which several smaller *States* agree to become members of a larger *one*, which they intend to form. It is a kind of assemblage of societies, that constitute a new one, capable of increasing by means of new associations, until they arrive to such a degree of power as to be able to provide for the security of the united body."[23] Madison, therefore, relied in part on the same passage from *The Spirit of the Laws* as Wilson.

Although Madison was very much influenced by Montesquieu, it is clear he did not agree with Montesquieu's view that republics need to be small in size to survive. However, in order to secure the support of the Anti-Federalists—as opposition to the Constitution was organizing in a number of states, some states were adding their own amendments to the Constitution with their ratification votes, and the Constitution's ratification was in doubt—the Federalists agreed that several amendments to the Constitution would be offered in the 1st Congress and thereafter to the states for ratification should the Constitution be adopted. Indeed, after its ratification in 1789, when the 1st Congress met, Madison drafted and became a leading advocate for the twelve amendments that were approved by Congress and sent to the states, of which ten were ratified—becoming the Bill of Rights.

It must be noted that the key figure urging a bill or declaration of rights from the earliest days was George Mason. Mason, a delegate from Virginia to the Constitutional Convention, was the author of the Virginia Declaration of Rights. Madison's draft of the Bill of Rights borrowed heavily from Mason's Virginia Declaration.

Importantly, not only did the Bill of Rights, and the earlier Virginia Declaration, incorporate John Locke's view of inalienable rights, providing one protection after another of the individual from government, but in the Tenth Amendment it sought to further address Montesquieu's concern respecting the difficulty of republican government succeeding in large countries and the Anti-Federalist objection that the Constitution created an overly centralized and powerful federal government that threatened state sovereignty.

The Tenth Amendment, which is very similar to Article 2 of the Articles of Confederation, provides that "[t]he powers not delegated to the United States by the Constitution, nor prohibited by it to the States, are reserved to the States respectively, or to the people."[24]

However, the Tenth Amendment, standing alone, did not completely satisfy the concerns about federal usurpation of state sovereignty. The Ninth Amendment was also crucial. It was demanded by several states prior to the Constitution's earlier ratification and provides that "[t]he enumeration in the Constitution, of certain rights, shall not be construed to deny or disparage others retained by the people."[25] The Ninth Amendment was to be read in conjunction with the Tenth Amendment.

In fact, in his speech against the constitutionality of the Bank of the United States on February 2, 1791, Madison specifically addressed the Ninth and Tenth amendments (originally the eleventh and twelfth amendments as proposed to the states for ratification), referring to them as "explanatory amendments"— that is, as Professor Kurt T. Lash explained, providing "the proper rule of interpretation, implied in the structure of the Constitution, represented by the Federalists to the state conventions, and demanded to be made express by those same conventions. . . ."[26]

Madison reasoned: "The explanatory amendments proposed by Congress themselves, at least, would be good authority with them [the state proposals]; all these renunciations of power proceeded on a rule of construction, excluding the latitude now contended for [in establishing the Bank of the United States]. These explanations were the more to be respected, as they had not only been proposed by Congress, but ratified by nearly three-fourths of the states. He read several of the articles proposed, remarking particularly on the 11th and 12th. [T]he former, as guarding against a latitude of interpretation—the latter, as excluding every source of power not within the constitution itself."[27] Madison concluded: "[I]f the power were in the constitution, the immediate exercise of it cannot be essential—if not there, the exercise of it involves the guilt of usurpation, and establishes a precedent of interpretation, levelling all the barriers which limit the powers of the general government, and protect those of the state governments."[28]

The Ninth and Tenth amendments, treated as mostly superfluous today, were fundamental to the Constitution's ratification and interpretation. Moreover, it is undeniable that the Constitution would not have been ratified but for a bill of rights, including these two amendments. Clearly, the most consequential Anti-Federalists and Federalists, at the federal and state levels, were of one mind in securing state sovereignty and preventing the federal government from evolving into a centralized despotism. Separation of powers, the enumeration of powers, and the explicit provision for state sovereignty were essential characteristics of the new constitutional republic.

LEGISLATORS

In determining the makeup of Congress, after much debate the delegates agreed to "The Great Compromise," offered by Roger Sherman of Connecticut, in which the members of the House of Representatives would be selected on the basis of the population within the states, and the members of the Senate would be selected by the states based on equal representation.

Article 1, Section 2, Clause 1 of the Constitution provides: "The House of Representatives shall be composed of Members chosen every second Year by the People of the several States, and the Electors in each State shall have the Qualifications requisite for Electors of the most numerous Branch of the State Legislature."

Article 1, Section 3, Clause 1: "The Senate of the United States shall be composed of two Senators from each State, chosen by the Legislature thereof, for six Years; and each Senator shall have one Vote."

Although Montesquieu favored proportional representation, his observation respecting proportional and equal representation within a national legislature was known to the delegates and obviously influenced their design. Montesquieu wrote, "It is unlikely that the states that associate will be of the same size and have equal power. The republic of the Lycians was an association of twenty-three towns; the large ones had three votes in the common council; the medium-sized ones, two; the small ones, one. The republic of Holland is composed of seven provinces, large and small, each having one vote" (2, 9, 3).

JUDGES

Montesquieu was adamant that a republican government required a judiciary unencumbered by the political pressures and influences of the legislature and executive but faithful to the text of the laws the legislature composed when exercising its adjudicative duties. "The power of judging should not be given to a permanent senate but should be exercised by persons drawn from the body of the people at certain times of the year in the manner prescribed by law to form a tribunal which lasts only as long as necessity requires. . . . But though tribunals should not be fixed, judgments should be fixed to such a degree that they are never anything but a precise text of the law. If judgments were the individual opinion of a judge, one would live in this society without knowing precisely what engagements one has contracted" (2, 2, 6).

The Constitution created the Supreme Court and granted Congress the power to create inferior courts. *Article 3, Section 1, Clause 1* of the Constitution provides: "The judicial Power of the United States, shall be vested in one supreme Court, and in such inferior Courts as the Congress may from time to time ordain and establish. The Judges, both of the supreme and inferior Courts, shall hold their Offices during good Behavior. . . ."

Filling the Supreme Court and the lower Article 3 courts would be a joint endeavor between the executive and the Senate (which was originally intended to represent the states), ensuring that no justice or judge would be beholden to one or the other political branches. The president would nominate judicial candidates and the Senate would consent, or reject them. *Article 2, Section 2,*

Clause 2 provides: He [the president] shall . . . nominate, and by and with the Advice and Consent of the Senate, . . . Judges of the supreme Court, and all other Officers of the United States, whose Appointments are not herein otherwise provided for, and which shall be established by Law. . . ."

COMMERCE

Montesquieu's view of the beneficial effects of private property and commerce in a republic was also shared by the delegates. As Montesquieu explained, "[T]he spirit of commerce brings with it the spirit of frugality, economy, moderation, work, wisdom, tranquility, order, and rule. . . ." (1, 5, 6) "Commerce cures destructive prejudices, and it is an almost general rule that everywhere there are gentle mores, there is commerce and that everywhere there is commerce, there are gentle mores. . . ." (4, 20, 1) "In short, one's belief that one's prosperity is more certain in these states makes one undertake everything, and because one believes that what one has acquired is secure, one dares to expose it in order to acquire more; only the means for acquisition are at risk; now, men expect much of their fortune. . . ." (4, 20, 4)

Indeed, during the convention debates Madison noted that the predatory and retaliatory taxation visited on some states by their neighbors was an endless source of "dissatisfaction and discord" and resulted in "New Jersey, placed between Philadelphia & N. York, [being] likened to a cask tapped at both ends; and N. Carolina, between Virginia & S. Carolina to a patient bleeding at both arms." [29] The Framers adopted language intended to overcome these obstacles to commerce. *Article I, Section 8, Clause 3* of the Constitution provides: "[The Congress shall have Power] To regulate Commerce with foreign Nations, and among the several States, and with the Indian tribes. . . ." This clause is often referred to as the Commerce Clause since it was intended to promote the trading of goods between and among states and eliminate state barriers to interstate commerce, extend prosperity and tranquility throughout the republic, and regulate commerce with foreign nations and Indian tribes.

Concomitant with promoting commerce, the Constitution protects private property from seizure by the government without a legitimate public purpose and fair compensation to the property owner. As part of the Bill of Rights, Congress approved, and the states ratified, the Fifth Amendment, which included the "Takings Clause" of the Constitution. It provides, "[N]or shall private property be taken [by the government] for public use, without just compensation."

Obviously, there is much more to the Constitution and the events surrounding it. But the purpose here is to highlight the most important areas of Montesquieu's influence on the Framers. Although he was not the only authority relied on by the Framers, his reach was momentous. Montesquieu's dread of despotism, commitment to political liberty, and keen intellect in analyzing both, together with his genius in applying philosophy to the mechanics of politics, were essential guideposts in establishing the Constitution and the American republic.

After fighting and winning a long, bloody, and costly revolution, it was certainly conceivable, or at least theoretically possible, that rather than join together to improve and then discard the Articles of Confederation for a new constitution, the Founders, many with different and conflicting notions of the particulars and nuances of governance and aligned with one or another faction, could have abandoned the process of establishing a federal government altogether. Moreover, history bursts with examples of triumphant democratic revolutions and movements hijacked by self-aggrandizing masterminds, who then commit their societies to tyrannical purposes; or the victorious dividing the spoils of a war won and taking for themselves power and wealth. But through it all, the Founders maintained their integrity and remained true to the revolution's purposes. None of the states were compelled to join the union, but all did. And the debates and decisions in the Constitutional Convention and the state ratifying conventions were always about the best ways to protect and promote the civil society and the liberties and rights of the individual, as enshrined in the Declaration of Independence. Indeed, with Montesquieu's *The Spirit of the Laws* as an outstanding reference, never before had a nation been so thoroughly engaged in such an extraordinary venture.

It is obvious that at every turn, the Constitution's Framers repudiated by words and actions—as did Montesquieu and Locke—the utopian designs of Plato's *Republic*, More's *Utopia*, and Hobbes's *Leviathan*, all of which had been known to them. Although Marx's *Communist Manifesto* would come later, the debates and decisions of the Framers, and the Constitution itself, make abundantly clear that they would have been no more enticed by the dogma of the "workers' paradise" than by any other form of tyranny disguised as utopia.

CHAPTER TEN

ALEXIS DE TOCQUEVILLE AND
DEMOCRACY IN AMERICA

ALEXIS DE TOCQUEVILLE WAS a French thinker and philosopher who lived from 1805 to 1859, and was greatly influenced
by Montesquieu. He wrote *Democracy in America*, which actually combines two volumes—the first written in 1835 and the
second written in 1840—based on his travels around America.
Whereas Locke and Montesquieu, among others, provided the
essential intellectual guidance to America's Founders and Framers, Tocqueville's insightful observations about democracy, and
particularly the American Republic, several decades after its establishment, are prescient predictions about both the strengths of
the American character as well as the allure and peril of what I
broadly and repeatedly describe as utopianism.

VOLUME I

Tocqueville wrote, "Many important observations suggest themselves upon the social condition of the Anglo-Americans; but there is one that takes precedent of all the rest. The social condition of the Americans is eminently democratic; this was its character at the foundation of the colonies, and it is still more strongly marked at the present day."[1]

He observed, "In America the aristocratic element has always been feeble from its birth; and if at the present day it is not actually destroyed, it is at any rate so completely disabled that we can scarcely assign to it any degree of influence on the course of affairs. The democratic principle, on the contrary, has gained so much strength by time, by events, and by legislation, as to have become not only predominant, but all-powerful. No family or corporate authority can be perceived; very often one cannot even discover in it any very lasting individual influence" (I, 52–53).

In America, Tocqueville saw equality, properly comprehended— that is, in the context of inalienable rights—and as practiced nowhere else. "America, then, exhibits in her social state an extraordinary phenomenon. Men are there seen on a greater equality in point of fortune and intellect, or, in other words, more equal in their strength, than in any other country of the world, or in any age of which history has perceived the remembrance" (I, 53).

Tocqueville explained, however, that the danger threatening yet motivating most societies is the miscomprehension of equality, resulting in their descent into centralized tyranny. Rather than embracing equality as a condition of natural law and inalienable rights, which underlie a free and diverse society, equality is misapplied politically in the form of radical egalitarianism and to promote equal social and economic outcomes. "There is, in fact, a manly and lawful passion for equality that incites men to wish all to be powerful and honored. This passion tends to elevate the humble to the rank of the great; but there exists also in the human heart a depraved taste for equality, which impels the weak to attempt to lower the powerful to their own level and reduces men to prefer equality in slavery to inequality with freedom. Not that those nations whose social condition is democratic naturally despise liberty; on the contrary, they have an instinctive love of it. But liberty is not the chief and constant object of their desires; equality is their idol: they make rapid and sudden efforts to obtain liberty and, if they miss their aim, resign themselves to their disappointment; but nothing can satisfy them without equality, and they would rather perish than lose it. . . ." (I, 53–54)

But the strength of the sovereignty of the American people, Tocqueville argued, helps arrest the usual and historic rise of tyranny. He explained: "The Anglo-Americans are the first nation who, having been exposed to this formidable alternative, have been happy enough to escape the dominion of absolute power. They have been allowed by their circumstances, their origin, their intelligence, and especially by their morals to establish and maintain the sovereignty of the people" (I, 54).

Tocqueville added that for Americans, the sovereignty of the people is deep-rooted and widespread. By this he meant that Americans have a say in, and are actively involved in, all aspects of their society. The sovereignty of the people includes their influence over their government, but it is bigger than that. It resonates throughout the culture. It is a mind-set. "Whenever the political laws of the United States are to be discussed, it is with the doctrine of the sovereignty of the people that we must begin. . . . In America the principle of the sovereignty of the people is neither barren nor concealed, as it is with some other nations; it is recognized by the customs and proclaimed by the laws; it spreads freely, and arrives without impediment at its most remote consequences. If there is a country in the world where the doctrine of the sovereignty of the people can be fairly appreciated, where it can be studied in its application to the affairs of society, and where its dangers and its advantages may be judged, that country is assuredly America" (I, 55).

The American society—the personality of its people and their spirit—is everywhere. It is vibrant and ingrained. America's government is not coercive or repressive, Tocqueville argued, because it reflects and respects the temperament and disposition of the people, including their traditions, customs, experiences, and mores. The people would tolerate no less. "In some countries a power exists which, though it is in a degree foreign to the social body, directs it, and forces it to pursue a certain track. In others the ruling force is divided, being partly within and partly without the ranks of the people. But nothing of the kind is to be seen in the United States; there society governs itself for itself. All power centers in its bosom, and scarcely an individual is to be met with who would venture to conceive or, still less, to express the idea of seeking it elsewhere. The nation participates in the making of its laws by the choice of its legislators, and in the execution of them by the choice of the agents of the executive government; it may almost be said to govern itself, so feeble and so restricted is the share left to the administration, so little do the authorities forget their popular origin and the power from which they emanate. The people reign in the American political world as the Deity does in the universe. They are the cause and aim of all things; everything comes from them, and everything is absorbed in them" (I, 58).

Consequently, Tocqueville observed, the American government is nothing like the governments in Europe, where the latter governments are central to European societies and lord over them, where their societies are formed and directed by their governments, and where their histories and experiences are far different in that they include life under tyrannies. In America, the government is innocuous and dispersed—that is, society does not evolve around the government. "Nothing is more striking to a European traveler in the United States than the absence of what we term the government, or the administration. Written laws exist in America, and one sees the daily execution of them; but although everything moves regularly, the mover can nowhere be discovered. The hand that directs the social machine is invisible. Nevertheless, as all persons must have recourse to certain grammatical forms, which are the foundation of human language, in order to express their thoughts; so all communities are obliged to secure their existence by submitting to a certain amount of authority, without which they fall into anarchy. This authority may be distributed in several ways, but it must always exist somewhere. . . ." (I, 70) "The administrative power in the United States presents nothing either centralized or hierarchical in its constitution; this accounts for its passing unperceived. The power exists, but its representative is nowhere to be seen" (I, 71).

Tocqueville observed that the shape of the American govern-

ment, especially and prominently its decentralization of governmental authority, was designed with forethought and intended to
preserve and secure the existing American society. "Division of
authority between the Federal government and the states—The
government of the states is the rule, the Federal government the
exception. . . . The obligation and the claims of the Federal government were simple and easily definable because the Union had
been formed with the express purpose of meeting certain great
general wants; but the claims and obligations of the individual
states, on the other hand, were complicated and various because
their government had penetrated into all the details of social life.
The attributes of the Federal government were therefore carefully
defined, and all that was not included among them was declared to
remain to the governments of the several states. Thus the government of the states remained the rule, and that of the confederation
was the exception" (I, 114–15).

Notwithstanding the authority of federal courts to decide disputes between the federal and state governments, Tocqueville
concluded that federal judges were well aware of the limits placed
on the federal government vis-à-vis the states. "It is true, the
Constitution had laid down the precise limits of the Federal supremacy; but whenever this supremacy is contested by one of the
states, a Federal tribunal decides the question. Nevertheless, the
dangers with which the independence of the states is threatened
by this mode of proceeding are less serious than they appear to
be. . . . [I]n America the real power is vested in the states far more
than the Federal government" (I, 143). Therefore, Tocqueville argued, federal judges would refrain from abusing their public trust
by remaining faithful to the original intent of the Framers and the

federal government's constitutional limits. He wrote, "The Federal judges are conscious of the relative weakness of the power in whose name they act; and they are more inclined to abandon the right of jurisdiction in cases where the law gives it to them than to assert a privilege to which they have no legal claim" (I, 143). The point being that while federal judges are of the federal government, they are not detached from the character of American society, the history of the founding, and the purposes of the Constitution. Hence, if federal judges are virtuous, they are not a threat to the society for they will not use their positions to aggrandize the federal government and their own roles. In essence, Tocqueville is restating Montesquieu's case respecting representative government. Montesquieu wrote that "in a popular state there must be an additional spring, which is VIRTUE. . . . [I]n a popular government when the laws have ceased to be executed, as this can come only from the corruption of the republic, the state is already lost" (1, 3, 3). Montesquieu added, "There are two sorts of tyranny: a real one, which consists in the violence of the government, and one of opinion, which is felt when those who govern establish things that run counter to a nation's way of thinking" (3, 19, 3). For Tocqueville, tyranny of the judiciary was alien to American society.

Tocqueville marveled at America's seemingly endless hurdles to despotism. In addition to America's historical repudiation of, and foundational limits on, centralized governmental power, manifested, for the most part, in the official behavior of those holding federal office, the obstacles to democratic tyranny, where a majority or faction of the population might seek to impose its will on the whole society, appeared a very difficult undertaking.

"In the American republics the central government has never as yet busied itself except with a small number of objects, sufficiently prominent to attract its attention. The secondary affairs of society have never been regulated by its authority; and nothing has hitherto betrayed its desire of even interfering in them. The majority has become more and more absolute, but has not increased the prerogatives of the central government; those great prerogatives have been confined to a certain sphere; and although the despotism of the majority may be galling upon one point, it cannot be said to extend to all" (I, 271).

Besides, argued Tocqueville, the American people will not abide democratic despotism, and the federal government has no way to administratively impose it on the multiplicity of diverse governmental institutions that would resist its enforcement. Therefore it is unlikely to descend to such rule. "However the predominant party in the nation may be carried away by its passions, however ardent it may be in the pursuit of its project, it cannot oblige all the citizens to comply with its desires in the same manner and at the same time throughout the country. When the central government which represents that majority has issued a decree, it must entrust the execution of its will to agents over whom it frequently has no control and whom it cannot perpetually direct. The townships, municipal bodies, and counties form so many concealed breakwaters, which check or part the popular determination. If an oppressive law were passed, liberty would still be protected by the mode of executing the law; the majority cannot descend to the details and what may be called the puerilities of administrative tyranny. It does not even imagine that it can do so, for it has not a full consciousness of its authority. It knows only the extent of its natural powers, but is unacquainted with the art of increasing them" (I, 271 and 272). Tocqueville appears to concur with James Madison and the Federalists, less so with Montesquieu and the Anti-Federalists, that America's vast territory and diverse communities would strengthen a state-centric republican form of government, making consolidation of governmental power more difficult. However, he was also insistent, as was Montesquieu and all of the most consequential Founders and Framers, on the imperative of federalism.

Tocqueville explained more than once, however, that America's history and experiences are unique. "This point deserves attention; for if a democratic republic, similar to that of the United States, were ever founded in a country where the power of one man had previously established a centralized administration and had sunk it deep into the habits and the laws of the people, I do not hesitate to assert that in such a republic a more insufferable despotism would prevail than in any of the absolute monarchies of Europe; or, indeed, than any that could be found on this side of Asia" (I, 272).

VOLUME II

Again, Tocqueville warned against the despotism of politically misapplied or imposed equality of social and economic conditions and results. "[T]he vices which despotism produces are precisely those which equality fosters. These two things perniciously complete and assist each other. Equality places men side by side, unconnected by any common tie; despotism raises barriers to keep them asunder; the former predisposes them not to consider their fellow creatures, the latter makes general indifference a sort of public virtue" (II, 102).

Tocqueville lauded the American system as antithetical to radical egalitarianism, for it limits federal intervention to certain general matters of national consequence and leaves to local decision-making the countless minor affairs of communities. However, he also distinguished centralized government and egalitarianism from the common interests, shared values, and regular interactions that make "a people." Tocqueville wrote, "The Americans have combated by free institutions the tendency of equality to keep men asunder, and they have subdued it. The legislators of America did not suppose that a general representation of the whole nation would suffice to ward off a disorder at once so natural to the frame of democratic society and so fatal; they also thought that it would be well to infuse political life into each portion of the territory in order to multiply to an infinite extent opportunities of acting in concert for all the members of the community and to make them constantly feel their mutual dependence. The plan was a wise one. The general affairs of a country engage the attention only of leading politicians, who assemble from time to time in the same places; and as they often lose sight of each other afterwards, no lasting ties are established between them. But if the object be to have the local affairs of a district conducted by the men who reside there, the same persons are always in contact, and they are, in a manner, forced to be acquainted and to adapt themselves to one another" (II, 103). Moreover, local decision-making binds citizens together within communities, for they are more attentive and active in the affairs that directly affect them and the well-being of their neighbors. "Thus far more may be done by entrusting to the citizens the administration of minor affairs than by surrendering them in the public welfare and convincing them that they constantly stand in need of one another in order to provide for it. . . . Local freedom, then, which leads a great number of citizens to value the affection of their neighbors and of their kindred, perpetually brings men together and forces them to help one another in spite of the propensities that sever them" (II, 104).

While rightly decrying the despotism of radical egalitarianism, Tocqueville also recognized that the American economic system—with its voluntary commercial interactions and the individual's right to acquire and retain property—creates more wealth and opportunity for more people than any other system. Indeed, in America, there are no permanent social or economic classes condemning people to a life of poverty or ensuring for others great wealth for all time. As such, the American economic system encourages success and discourages as self-defeating the plundering of the successful. "I am aware that among a great democratic people there will always be some members of the community in great poverty and others in great opulence; but the poor, instead of forming the immense majority of the nation, as is always the case in aristocratic communities, are comparatively few in number, and the laws do not bind them together by the ties of irremediable and hereditary penury. . . . As there is no longer a race of poor men, so there is no longer a race of rich men; the latter spring up daily from the multitude and relapse into it again. Hence, they do not form a distinct class which may be easily marked out and plundered; and, moreover, as they are connected with the mass of their fellow citizens by a thousand secret ties, the people cannot assail them without inflicting an injury upon themselves" (II, 252).

Tocqueville observed that in America, the vast majority of people are neither poor nor rich, they desire but are not obsessed with becoming rich, and they are loyal to a stable yet free system in which they are able to benefit and have a financial stake. "Between the two extremes of democratic communities stands an innumerable multitude of men almost alike, who, without being exactly either rich or poor, possess sufficient property to desire the maintenance of order, yet not enough to excite envy. Such men are the natural enemies of violent commotions; their lack of agitation keeps all beneath them and above them still and secures the balance of the fabric of society. Not, indeed, that even these men are contented with what they have got or that they feel a natural abhorrence for a revolution in which they might share the spoil without sharing the calamity; on the contrary, they desire, with unexampled ardor, to get rich, but the difficulty is to know from whom riches can be taken. The same state of society that constantly prompts desires, restrains these desires within necessary limits; it gives men more liberty of changing, and less interest in change. Not only are the men of democracies not naturally desirous of revolutions, but they are afraid of them. All revolutions more or less threaten the tenure of property; but most of those who live in democratic countries are possessed of property; not only do they possess property, but they live in the condition where men set the greatest store upon their property" (II, 252–53). In essence, the pursuit and acquisition of private property is crucial to the maintenance of the civil society.

Tocqueville pointed out that in democracies there is a tendency for some who fall on hard times to submit voluntarily to government authority for their sustenance, seeing it as the only way out. However, as their reliance on government becomes more complete, Tocqueville argued, they do so proudly for they are no less considered citizens than those who do not submit to government authority. "As in periods of equality no man is compelled to lend his assistance to his fellow men, and none has any right to expect much support from them, everyone is at once independent and powerless. These two conditions, which must never be either separately considered or confounded together, inspire the citizen of a democratic country with very contrary propensities. His independence fills him with self-reliance and pride among his equals; his debility makes him feel from time to time the want of some outward assistance, which he cannot expect from any of them, because they are all impotent and unsympathizing. In this predicament he naturally turns his eyes to that imposing power which alone rises above the level of universal depression. Of that power his wants and especially his desires continually remind him, until he ultimately views it as the sole and necessary support of his own weakness. This may more completely explain what frequently takes place in democratic countries, where the very men who are so impatient of superiors patiently submit to a master, exhibiting at once their pride and their servility" (II, 294–95).

Even more, Tocqueville explained in greater detail that the tyranny that most endangers free societies is a soft tyranny. It is the gradual imposition of and acquiescence to radical egalitarianism, which is disguised as democratic and administrative utilitarianism. It is the belief in the infinite ability and capacity of elected officials to perfect life and in a vast, neutral administrative state to ensure its proper regulation. Tocqueville wrote, "Democratic governments may become violent and even cruel at certain periods of extreme effervescence or of great danger, but these crises will be rare and brief. When I consider the petty passions of our contemporaries, the mildness of their manners, the extent of their education, and purity of their religion, the gentleness of their morality, their regular and industrious habits, and the restraint which they almost all observe in their vices no less than in their virtues, I have no fear that they will meet tyrants in their rulers, but rather with their guardians" (II, 317–18).

He wrote further, "I think, then, that the species of oppression by which democratic nations are menaced is unlike anything that ever before existed in the world; our contemporaries will find no prototype of it in their memories. I seek in vain for an expression that will accurately convey the whole of the idea I have formed of it; the old words *despotism* and *tyranny* are inappropriate: the thing itself is new, and since I cannot name, I must attempt to define it" (II, 318). Actually, it may be different or novel in the particulars of its evolution and form, but the species is generally known. It is utopianism.

Tocqueville described a nation in which the civil society collapses. He wrote, "I seek to trace the novel features under which despotism may appear in the world. The first thing that strikes the observation is an innumerable multitude of men, all equal and alike, incessantly endeavoring to procure the petty and paltry pleasures with which they glut their lives. Each of them, living apart, is as a stranger to the fate of all the rest; his children and his private friends constitute to him the whole of mankind. As for the rest of his fellow citizens, he is close to them, but he does not see them; he touches them, but he does not feel them; he exists only in himself and for himself alone; and if his kindred still remain to him, he may be said at any rate to have lost his country" (II, 318).

With the people denuded of spirit and exceptionality, dependent on the government for their welfare, the democracy gradually transitions into a powerful administrative state. "Above this race of men stands an immense and tutelary power, which takes upon itself alone to secure their gratifications and to watch over their fate. That power is absolute, minute, regular, provident, and mild. It would be like the authority of a parent if, like that authority, its object was to prepare men for manhood; but it seeks, on the contrary, to keep them in perpetual childhood: it is well content that the people should rejoice, provided they think of nothing but rejoicing. For their happiness such a government willingly labors, but it chooses to be the sole agent and the only arbiter of that happiness; it provides for their security, foresees and supplies their necessities, facilitates their pleasures, manages their principal concerns, directs their industry, regulates the descent of property, and subdivides their inheritances; what remains, but to spare them all the care of thinking and all the trouble of living? Thus it every day renders the exercise of the free agency of man less useful and less frequent; it circumscribes the will within a narrower range and gradually robs a man of all the uses of himself. The principle of equality has prepared men for these things; it has predisposed men to endure them and often to look on them as benefits" (II, 318–19).

Tocqueville went on to portray the amorphousness and insatiableness of the administrative state, as it corrals, prods, and directs the individual at will in nearly all aspects of life, where existence becomes bleak and dark. "After having thus successively taken each member of the community in its powerful grasp and fashioned him at will, the supreme power then extends its arm over the whole community. It covers the surface of society with a network of small complicated rules, minute and uniform, through which the most original minds and the most energetic characters cannot penetrate, to rise above the crowd. The will of man is not shattered, but softened, bent, and guided; men are seldom forced by it to act, but they are constantly restrained from acting. Such a power does not destroy, but prevents existence; it does not tyr- annize, but it compresses, enervates, extinguishes, and stupefies a people, till each nation is reduced to nothing better than a flock of timid and industrious animals, of which the government is the shepherd" (II, 319).

Tocqueville then made the profound observation that this dreary existence is accepted by the people, for they go through the motions of electing their guardians, deluding themselves that they and their fellow citizens remain free for they participate in self-government. However, as the administrative state grows, the vote is less effective and the individual is increasingly disenfran- chised. "I have always thought that servitude of the regular, quiet, and gentle kind which I have just described might be combined more easily than is commonly believed with some of the outward forms of freedom, and that it might even establish itself under the wing of the sovereignty of the people" (II, 319). Elaborating on this point, he wrote, "Our contemporaries are constantly excited by two conflicting passions: they want to be led, and they wish to remain free. As they cannot destroy either the one or the other of these contrary propensities, they strive to satisfy them both at once. They devise a sole, tutelary, and all-powerful form of government, but elected by the people. They combine the principle of centralization and that of popular sovereignty; this gives them a respite; they console themselves for being in tutelage by the reflection that they have chosen their own guardians. Every man allows himself to be put in leading-strings, because he sees that it is not a person or a class of persons, but the people at large who hold the end of his chain. By this system the people shake off their state of dependence just long enough to select their master and then relapse into it again. A great many persons at present day are quite contented with this sort of compromise between administrative despotism and the sovereignty of the people; and they think they have done enough for the protection of individual freedom when they have surrendered it to the power of the nation at large. . . ." (II, 319)

In the end, Tocqueville explained, what is left is a hollowed-out democracy consumed by administrative absolutism, against which there is little resistance. "Subjection in minor affairs breaks out every day and is felt by the whole community indiscriminately. It does not drive men to resistance, but it crosses them at every turn, till they are led to surrender the exercise of their own will. Thus their spirit is gradually broken and their character enervated; whereas that obedience which is exacted on a few important but rare occasions only exhibits servitude at certain intervals and throws the burden of it upon a small number of men. It is in vain to summon a people who have been rendered so dependent on the central power to choose from time to time the representatives of that power; this rare and brief exercise of their free choice, however important it may be, will not prevent them from gradually losing the faculties of thinking, feeling, and acting for themselves, and thus gradually falling below the level of humanity" (II, 319–20).

The irony is not lost on Tocqueville. "The democratic nations that have introduced freedom into their political constitution at the very time when they were augmenting the despotism of their administrative constitution have been led into strange paradoxes. To manage those minor affairs in which good sense is all that is wanted, the people are held to be unequal to the task; but when the government of the country is at stake, the people are invested with immense powers; they are alternately made the playthings of their rule, and his masters, more than kings and less than men. . . . It is indeed difficult to conceive how men who have entirely given up the habit of self-government should succeed in making a proper choice of those by whom they are to be governed; and no one will ever believe that a liberal, wise, and energetic government can spring from the suffrages of a subservient people" (II, 321).

In America, however, Tocqueville believed he found a different kind of democracy. Although still fraught with challenges and dangers, as Tocqueville warned repeatedly, and requiring the watchful and active resolve of the people, at the core of American society Tocqueville saw a conviction in the sovereignty of the individual and the people generally, unique in world history. Tocqueville observed that of all societies likely to effectively resist the soft tyranny that overtakes democracies, America would be that society. He believed that the American people would not be easily tempted by radical egalitarianism, dispirited, and willingly ruled over by a centralized governing authority, whether the tyranny of a single despot or an elected assembly and its administrative state, even in the unlikely event such an effort should be attempted. The history, traditions, experience, and mores of the American people, and their love of freedom, independence, pride, and self-sufficiency—as well as the breadth and diversity of American society, with its multitude of local governing bodies—would seem to make such an undertaking impracticable if not impossible. Tocqueville noted that the American constitution itself is a document of forethought and purpose, imposing detailed and defined limits and obstacles on the federal government, and beyond them, walling society from it.

Still, Tocqueville knew that the governing despotism of which he wrote, and which can accurately and broadly be characterized as utopianism, is, for free men, living in civil societies, a perpetual and existential threat—even in America. In the end, he wondered if any democracy could withstand it. He concluded that ultimately it is up to the people. They will decide whether they shall be free or not. "I am full of apprehensions and hopes. I perceive mighty dangers which it is possible to ward off, mighty evils which may be avoided or alleviated; and I cling with a firmer hold to the belief that for democratic nations to be virtuous and prosperous, they require but to will it. . . . The nations of our time cannot prevent the conditions of men from becoming equal, but it depends upon themselves whether the principle of equality is to lead them to servitude or freedom, to knowledge or barbarism, to prosperity or wretchedness" (II, 334).

PART III

ON UTOPIANISM
AND
AMERICANISM

CHAPTER ELEVEN

POST-CONSTITUTIONAL AMERICA

WHEN JOHN LOCKE WROTE about the nature of man in the state of nature, he faced skepticism from some contemporaries. But his description was not theoretical. Indeed, not only was his influence on the American founding significant, but he rightly pointed to America as evidence for his observations and conclusions that individual self-interest and self-preservation, the right to life and liberty, the use of labor to improve and possess property, and equality in justice formed the natural state of human existence. And the quality of this existence promotes industriousness, sociability, civility, economic prosperity, and charity among men. "Everyone as he is bound to preserve himself, and not to quit his station willfully, so by the like reason, when his own preservation comes not in competition, ought he as much as he can to preserve the rest of mankind, and not unless it be to do justice on an offender, take away or impair the life or what tends the preservation of the life, the liberty, health, limb, or goods of another" (*Second Treatise*, 2, 6). "It is often asked as a mighty objection, where are, or ever were, there any men in such a state of Nature? . . . The promises and bargains for truck [trade], etc. . . . in the woods of America, are binding to them, though they are perfectly in a state of Nature in reference to one another for truth, and keeping the faith belongs to men as men, and not as members of society" (2, 14).

Concisely put, this is the heritage and lineage of the American people, which dates hundreds of years before the American Revolution and transcends all else. From the earliest settlers escaping persecution or seeking opportunities in the New World, to the original colonies asserting self-rule through popular sovereignty and numerous local governing bodies; from the demand for independence, the assertion of inalienable individual rights, and the Revolutionary War, to the founding of the constitutional republic to secure individual liberty and the civil society, the American people engaged in the most widely considered and far-reaching exploration of humanity—its meaning, cultivation, and application—in world history. Even half a century after the adoption of the Constitution, the character and psychology of the American people were apparent to Alexis de Tocqueville, who wrote, "They have been allowed by their circumstances, their origin, their intelligence, and especially by their morals to establish and maintain the sovereignty of the people" (*Democracy in America*, I, 54).

When the fifty-five delegates met in Philadelphia in 1787 at what became known as the Constitutional Convention, their purpose was not to transform American society but to preserve and protect it. In *Federalist* 51, James Madison later explained the decisive task this way: "But what is government itself, but the greatest of all reflections on human nature? If men were angels, no government would be necessary. If angels were to govern men, neither external nor internal controls on government would be necessary. In framing a government which is to be administered by men over men, the great difficulty lies in this: you must first enable the government to control the governed and in the next place oblige it to control itself." Charles de Montesquieu's advice guided the Framers. He wrote that laws "should relate to the degree of liberty that the constitution can sustain, to the religion of the inhabitants, their inclinations, their wealth, their number, their commerce, their mores, and their manners. . . ." (*Spirit of the Laws*, 1, 1, 3)

The debates between the Federalist and Anti-Federalist camps did not involve fundamental disagreements about the nature of man and inalienable rights, about which there was near-universal consent and for which a revolution had been fought and won, but how best to arrange a government, after the revolution, to ensure the perpetuation of American society. The delegates at the constitutional and state conventions feared above all else the concentration of too much power in the new federal government. In fact, at the Constitutional Convention, the delegates specifically considered and rejected a proposal by Delaware's Gunning Bedford for a broad grant of power to Congress to pass laws of general interest, or where states might be said to be incompetent, or where state action might be said to disrupt the harmony of the nation. Although the delegates sought to establish a federal government that would overcome the deficiencies of the Articles of Confederation, Bedford went much too far. Virginia's Edmund Randolph objected that under Bedford's scheme, state constitutions and laws would be of no consequence and Congress could intervene at will in state affairs.[1] Bedford's proposal went nowhere.

Not only was there no support for an all-powerful central government, but the delegates at the Constitutional Convention spent most of the summer trying to figure out how to ensure that no office or officeholder in the new federal government would become too powerful. As is well-known, they separated powers between and among the legislative, executive, and judicial branches and enumerated the powers within each branch in considerable detail.

The delegates also opposed majoritarianism in its purest forms for it encouraged factionalism and threatened individual sovereignty, should a group or majority succeed in controlling the government and imposing their will on society. Consequently, the only direct elections would occur in selecting members of the House of Representatives; senators would be chosen by the states; although the people would vote for president, the president would ultimately be elected by members of an electoral college; and judicial candidates would be nominated by the president for confirmation or rejection by the Senate.

The Framers believed they had done what they could, through the Constitution, to fend off tyranny by the few and the many.

Still, the Anti-Federalists were not convinced, and ratification of the Constitution in several states was in jeopardy. Madison and others tried to alleviate the objections. In *Federalist* 39, Madison argued that the federal government had only "certain enumerated" powers and the states retained "residuary and inviolable sovereignty" over all else.[2] In *Federalist* 45, he asserted that the

proposed federal powers were "few and limited" and the power in
the states remained "numerous and indefinite."[3] Nonetheless, Virginia's George Mason, among many others, insisted that more was
needed to contain federal authority and safeguard the states' plenary power. In order to secure the Constitution's ratification, the
Federalists eventually agreed to introduce a set of amendments in
the 1st Congress, which had been widely accepted in advance,
further delineating and underscoring the limits of the federal government respecting its potential abuse against the individual and
usurpation of the states. They became known as the Bill of Rights.

Much has changed in America, and for the worse. I am not
speaking of the natural change, evolution, and progress that flows
from spontaneous interactions among free people, which is mostly
desirable, essential, and regular. In fact, it is the disposition of the
civil society. It is the reason for advancements and developments
in new products, services, technologies, science, medicine, etc.,
and the source of the nation's economic vibrancy and prosperity. Contrarily, the underlying factors and values that make possible the civil society, which center on the liberty and rights of
the individual, have been and are being devitalized and stifled by
utopian masterminds who substitute their preferences, objectives,
and decisions—including rewarding their political allies and
supporters—for a free people.

The means by which these utopians amass their power is
through the federal government. The federal government has become unmoored from its origins. As a result, America today is not
strictly a constitutional republic, because the Constitution has
been and continues to be easily altered by a judicial oligarchy that
mostly enforces, if not expands, federal power. It is not strictly a

representative republic, because so many edicts are produced by
a maze of administrative departments that are unknown to the
public and detached from its sentiment. It is not strictly a federal republic, because the states that gave the central government
life now live at its behest. America is becoming, and in significant ways has become, a post-constitutional, democratic utopia
of sorts. It exists behind a Potemkin-like image of constitutional
republicanism. Its essential elements and unique features are being ingurgitated by an insatiable federal government that seeks to
usurp and displace the civil society.

Montesquieu warned of government's threat to civil society
unless it follows a moderate course. "May we be left as we are, said
a gentleman of [a republican government]. Nature repairs everything" (3, 19, 6). Tocqueville believed that America had, effect,
heeded Montesquieu's counsel. "Nothing is more striking to a European traveler in the United States than the absence of what we
term the government, or the administration. . . . The administrative power in the United States presents nothing either centralized or hierarchical in its constitution; this accounts for its passing
unperceived. . . ." (I, 70–71) However, that was then. America
has been transitioning from a society based on God-given inalienable rights protective of individual and community sovereignty
to a centralized, administrative statism that has become a power
unto itself. It appears nearly everywhere as a dominant fixture and
intrusive force in daily life. If its interventions are with limits,
the limits are increasingly difficult to define. The circle of liberty,
which was once expansive, and within which the individual was
largely unmolested in his manner and pursuits, is shrinking rapidly
as less and less area is left for him to live without torment.

The architects of America's unmaking are too numerous

to list, let alone examine with particularity. However, the most prominent include Woodrow Wilson, who merits at least brief attention.

In 1908, as president of Princeton University and prior to ascending to the Oval Office in 1913, Wilson authored a treatise titled *Constitutional Government in the United States*. Yet, Wilson wrote not of the Constitution as is but as he wished it to be—that is, denuded of its carefully crafted limits on the central government.

Wilson asserted, "No doubt a great deal of nonsense has been talked about the inalienable rights of the individual, and a great deal that was mere vague sentiment and pleasing speculation has been put forward as fundamental principle."[4] Clearly, Wilson dismissed not only the Declaration of Independence and the Founders' announced purpose for American independence, but the Lockean exposition on natural law, the nature of man, the social compact establishing the civil society, and the essential ingredients of constitutional republicanism (shared broadly by most of the best thinkers of the European Enlightenment). In short, for Wilson, rights are awarded or denied the individual as determined by the government.

Underscoring this point, Wilson argued, "Government is a part of life, and, with life, it must change, alike in its objects and in its practices; only this principle must remain unaltered,—this principle of liberty, that there must be the freest right and opportunity of adjustment. Political liberty consists in the best practicable adjustment between the power of the government and the privilege of the individual; and the freedom to alter the adjustment is as important as the adjustment itself for the ease and progress of affairs and the contentment of the citizen."[5] Notice Wilson's use of the

word *privilege* in lieu of *inalienable rights* when discussing the status
of the individual in his utopia, underscoring the malleability of
rights at the hands of masterminds.

For Wilson, government is to be treated as a living being; indeed, it is the most important of beings. Identifying man with the
state and the state with man is typical of utopians. In the *Republic*,
Plato wrote that "a just man won't differ at all from a just city in
respect to the form of justice; rather he'll be like the city" (435b).
Thus man ought not fear government but surrender to it, embrace
it, and be at one with it. The Framers' efforts to restrict federal
power with checks and balances, etc., would, in Wilson's view, deprive oxygen to the body of government just as assuredly as would
restricting the various organs of man.

In furtherance of this analogy, Wilson wrote, "It is difficult to
describe any single part of a great governmental system without
describing the whole of it. Governments are living things and operate as organic wholes. Moreover, governments have their natural
evolution and are one thing in one age, another in another. The
makers of the Constitution constructed the federal government
upon a theory of checks and balances which was meant to limit
the operation of each part and allow to no single part or organ of
it a dominating force; but no government can be successfully conducted upon so mechanical a theory. Leadership and control must
be lodged somewhere; the whole art of statesmanship is the art of
bringing the several parts of government into effective cooperation for the accomplishment of particular common objects, and
party objects at that. Our study of each part of our federal system,
if we are to discover our real government as it lives, must be made
to disclose to us its operative coordination as a whole: its places of

leadership, its method of action, how it operates, what checks it, what gives it energy and effect. Governments are what politicians make them, and it is easier to write of the President than of the presidency."[6]

Wilson took direct aim at Montesquieu as the source of the Framers' single-minded and supposedly misplaced reliance on divided government. "The makers of our federal Constitution followed the scheme as they found it expounded in Montesquieu, followed it with genuine scientific enthusiasm. The admirable expositions of the *Federalist* read like thoughtful applications of Montesquieu to the political needs and circumstances of America. They are full of the theory of checks and balances. The President is balanced off against Congress, Congress against the President, and each against the courts. Our statesmen of the earlier generations quoted no one so often as Montesquieu, and they quoted him always as a scientific standard in the field of politics. Politics is turned into mechanics under his touch. . . ."[7]

Wilson's objective was to centralize and consolidate power in the federal government and redefine the relationship between it and the individual. His assignation of human characteristics to the federal government was an argument for maximalist federal power where the central government has unrestrained flexibility and freedom to operate, and where the rights of actual human beings are diminished and their pursuits restricted. The individual lives to serve the body politic and, in turn, the politicians who oversee it. Wilson wrote, "The trouble with the theory [of limited, divided government] is that government is not a machine, but a living thing. . . . It is modified by its environment, necessitated by its tasks, shaped to its functions by the sheer pressure of life. No living thing can have its organs offset against each other as checks, and live. On the contrary, its life is dependent upon their quick cooperation, their ready response to the commands of instinct or intelligence, their amicable community of purpose. Government is not a body of blind forces; it is a body of men, with highly differentiated functions, no doubt, in our modern day of specialization, but with a common task and purpose. Their cooperation is indispensable, their warfare fatal. There can be no successful government without leadership or without the intimate, almost instinctive, coordination of the organs of life and action. This is not theory, but fact, and displays its force as fact, whatever theories may be thrown across its track. Living political constitutions must be Darwinian in structure and in practice."[8] Wilson's reference to Darwinism highlights his notion of the federal government in a constant state of motion and evolution, where the Constitution and the government it establishes are no longer fixed or predictable. The individual and society generally are to serve the nutritional demands for eternal governmental growth, in the form of power, demanded by Wilson's utopian dogma.

Wilson would substitute Locke's civil society and Montesquieu's limits on government with a form of Thomas Hobbes's social compact. In describing his "great Leviathan," Hobbes argued, "Every man should say to every man *I authorize and give up my right of governing myself to this man, or to this assembly of men, on this condition, that thou give up thy right to him, and authorize all his actions in a like manner.*" "That *Mortal God* to which we owe, under the *Immortal God*, our peace and defence." And in this Sovereign "consisteth the essence of the commonwealth, which is *one person, of whose acts a great multitude, by mutual covenants one with another, have made themselves every one the author, to the end he may use the strength and means of them all, as he shall think expedient, for their peace and common defence*" (*Leviathan*, 109). For Wilson, the federal government, and particularly the president, takes on the qualities of Hobbes's Sovereign. Indeed, Wilson proclaimed, "the President is at liberty, both in law and conscience, to be as big a man as he can. His capacity will set the limit; and if Congress be overborne by him, it will be no fault of the makers of the Constitution,—it will be from no lack of constitutional powers on its part, but only because the President has the nation behind him, and Congress has not."[9] There are few demagogues and tyrants who would disagree with such a prescription.

Wilson argued further, as he had to, that the federal courts are not bound to the Constitution. "The weightiest import of the matter is seen only when it is remembered that the courts are the instruments of the nation's growth, and that the way in which they serve that use will have much to do with the integrity of every national process. If they determine what powers are to be exercised under the Constitution, they by the same token determine also the adequacy of the Constitution in respect of the needs and interests of the nation; our conscience in matters of law and our opportunity in matters of politics are in their hands."[10] Moreover, the only legitimate opinions the federal courts can render are those that endorse and promote the expansion of federal power. "[T]hat if they had interpreted the Constitution in its strict letter, as some proposed, and not in its spirit, like the charter of a business corporation and not like the charter of a living government, the vehicle of a nation's life, it would have proved a straight-jacket, a means not of liberty and development, but of mere restriction and embarrassment."[11]

What, then, should guide federal judges if not the Constitution? Apparently their uniquely innate wisdom. Wilson wrote, "What we should ask of our judges is that they prove themselves such men as can discriminate between the opinion of the moment and the opinion of the age, between the opinion which springs, a legitimate essence, from the enlightened judgment of men of thought and good conscience, and the opinion of desire, self-interest, of impulse and impatience."[12]

Therefore, the purpose of the judiciary is to sanction, if not clear the path for, the extraconstitutional actions of the federal Leviathan, especially the president. Wilson argued for a judicial oligarchy that would, in essence, sanction the rewriting of the Constitution in accordance with his utopian belief in what Plato characterized in the *Republic* as an Ideal City. In fact, so difficult are the Constitution's amendment processes that the courts are encouraged to circumvent them and to be praised when they do. "The character of the process of constitutional adaptation depends first of all upon the wise or unwise choice of statesmen, but ultimately and chiefly upon the option and purpose of the courts. The chief instrumentality by which the law of the Constitution has been extended to cover the facts of national development has of course been judicial interpretation,—the decisions of the courts. The process of formal amendment of the Constitution was made so difficult by the provisions of the Constitution itself that it has seldom been feasible to use it; and the difficulty of formal amendment has undoubtedly made the courts more liberal, not to say more lax, in their interpretation than they would otherwise have been. The whole business of adaptation has been theirs, and they have undertaken it with open minds, sometimes even with boldness and a touch of audacity. . . ."[13]

Even Tocqueville misjudged the federal judiciary's capacity for steamrolling its way through the Constitution and society. He wrote, "It is true, the Constitution had laid down the precise limits of the Federal supremacy; but whenever this supremacy is contested by one of the states, a Federal tribunal decides the question. Nevertheless, the dangers with which the independence of the states is threatened by this mode of proceeding are less serious than they appear to be. . . . [I]n America the real power is vested in the states far more than the Federal government." Tocqueville believed that "[t]he Federal judges are conscious of the relative weakness of the power in whose name they act; and they are more inclined to abandon the right of jurisdiction in cases where the law gives it to them than to assert a privilege to which they have no legal claim" (I, 143).

Furthermore, Wilson's utopianism necessarily grants Congress extensive and expanded power to legislate without regard to, or over the top of, the states. The entire federalist approach, so crucial during the founding and to the Framers of the Constitution, and without which there would have been no United States, must be demolished. "What, reading our Constitution, in its true spirit, neither sticking in its letter nor yet forcing it arbitrarily to mean what we wish it to mean, shall be the answer of our generation, pressed upon by gigantic economic problems the solution of which may involve not only the prosperity but also the very integrity of the nation, to the old question of the distribution of powers between Congress and the States?"[14] Notice Wilson's arrogance when he claims he is not insisting that the Constitution reflect "what we wish it to mean"—that is, what he wishes it to mean— but that he is simply revealing "its true spirit."

Of course, Wilson read the Ninth and Tenth amendments out of the Constitution, as they are the most explicit statement of individual and state sovereignty in the Constitution. His view has been adopted by most federal courts in modern times, using the Civil War and popular opinion as sham rationales for licensing unfettered federal authority. "The old theory of the sovereignty of the States, which used so to engage our passions, has lost its vitality. The war between the States established at least this principle, that the federal government is, through its courts, the final judge of its own powers."[15] Furthermore, "we are impatient of state legislatures because they seem to us less representative of the thoughtful opinion of the country than Congress is. We know that our legislatures do not think alike, but we are not sure that our people do not think alike. . . ."[16]

Wilson contended that this is all necessary and proper. Indeed, it is the inevitable tide of history and mankind's fate. "Undoubtedly the powers of the federal government have grown, have even grown enormously, since the creation of the government, and they have grown for the most part without amendment of the Constitution. But they have grown in almost every instance by a process which must be regarded as perfectly normal and legitimate. The Constitution cannot be regarded as a mere legal document, to be read as a will or a contract would be. It must, of the necessity of the case, be a vehicle of life. As the life of the nation changes so must the interpretation of the document which contains it change, by a nice adjustment, determined, not by the original intention of those who drew the paper, but by the exigencies and the new aspects of life itself. Changes of fact and alterations of opinion bring in their train actual extensions of community interest, actual additions to the catalogue of things which must be included under the general terms of the law. . . ."[17] Again, Hobbes would approve. As Hobbes wrote, "So that it appeareth plainly, to my understanding, both from reason and Scripture, that the sovereign power (whether placed in one man, as in monarchy, or in one assembly of men, as in popular and aristocratical commonwealths) is as great as possibly men can be imagined to make it. . . ." (135)

Throughout his treatise, Wilson used the lexicon of the Constitution to justify its deconstruction—a practice employed regularly by utopian masterminds today, including those who serve as judges and justices. He argued that the federal masterminds and their experts were best qualified to rule over the people, yet he simultaneously claimed they were most knowledgeable of and responsive to the opinion of the people—another rhetorical device adopted by modern utopian politicians and propagandists. Hobbes wrote, "Nothing the sovereign representative can do to the subject, on what pretence soever, can properly be called injustice, or injury, because every subject is author of every act the sovereign doth. . . ." (138)

Moreover, Wilson proved the insight of Madison's fear—that is, without the Constitution's limits on the federal government's authority, an election could empower a temporary majority or faction to fundamentally alter the governmental structure in ways that threaten the individual's liberty and rights. Furthermore, since the federal courts are free to exercise extraconstitutional power and, according to Wilson, have the final word, elections that deliver results contrary to utopian ambitions become largely inconsequential in containing or reversing those ambitions, for the masterminds, in the name of the people, can blunt or reverse them.

Wilson argued for obstructing every avenue for preserving or reestablishing constitutional primacy by corrupting the Constitution itself. Having emptied it of its original purpose, the Constitution would become the vessel into which the utopians pour their agenda. The president is to be as powerful as he can, the courts are to rewrite the Constitution at will, and the Congress is to rule over state legislatures without limits. The federal government, therefore, could never be tamed. Its utopian direction could not be effectively altered. The entire American enterprise would be corrupted. Montesquieu observed that "in a popular state there must be an additional spring, which is VIRTUE. What I say is confirmed by the entire body of history and is quite in conformity with the nature of things. . . . [I]n a popular government when the laws have ceased to be executed, as this can come only from the corruption of the republic, the state is already lost" (1, 3, 3). In despotic government, "virtue is not at all necessary to it. . . ." (1, 3, 8)

So perverse was Wilson's language and thinking that "virtue" would be defined by its opposite—deceit. Wilson advocated nothing short of a diabolical counterrevolution, by means of contorting the instrumentalities of government, to undo the purposes of the American Revolution. He sought to supplant the basic character of American society and the nation's founding with a supreme central government. The greater the liberty and flexibility of the federal government to act, the more debilitated the individual, for he is the focus of its designs. The individual is, in fact, lost in this scheme. Locke explained that "freedom from absolute, arbitrary power is so necessary to, and closely joined with, a man's preservation, that he cannot part with it but by what forfeits his preservation and life together. . . ." (4, 22)

A few decades later, Wilson's post-constitutional utopianism would serve as a blueprint for Franklin Roosevelt. Much like Wilson, before climbing to the presidency Roosevelt revealed his own contempt for the Constitution's limits on federal power. He, too, conflated the nature of civil society with the tyranny of unbridled government. Roosevelt also insisted that although the utopian counterrevolution was supported by most Americans, its full realization was thwarted by divisions among the utopians and obstructions by an intransigent conservative minority. In his 1926 *Whither Bound* address, Roosevelt argued, "In the methods of our governing . . . we have come to accept, or at least to discuss without fear, problems and methods formerly mentioned only by wild-eyed visionaries. . . . Probably on any given problem of modern life, if a count or classification could be made, the out-and-out conservatives would be found to be in a distant minority. Yet the majority would be so divided over the *means* by which to gain their ends that they could not present sufficient unity to obtain action. This has been the history of progress. . . . Measured by years the actual control of human affairs is in the hands of conservatives for longer periods than in those of liberals or radicals. When the latter do come into power, they translate the constantly working leaven of progress into law or custom or use, but rarely obtain enough time in control to make further economic or social experiments. None of us, therefore, need feel surprise that the government of our own country, for instance, is conservative by far the greater part of the time. Our national danger is, however, not that it may for four years or eight years become liberal or even radical, but that it may suffer from too long a period of the do-nothing or reactionary standards. Certainly it would appear on the surface that a natural advantage lies with those among us who dislike to see change. It is so much more easy to accept what we are told than to think things out for ourselves. It takes courage, too, to disagree with our everyday companions; the obvious path is simpler to follow than one of our own making." [18]

Roosevelt repositioned the utopians as enlightened, modern, and futuristic, and, conversely, presented the advocates of civil society and constitutionalism as obstructing individual and societal progress. "If, then, we realize that the days in which we live present great problems wholly new, we may adopt one of two attitudes. Some among us would stop the clock, call a halt in all this change, and then in some well-thought-out way bring back an orderly, defined method of life. Old standards and customs would revive to meet the new conditions, classic dicta would again govern—the 'good old days' restored. It is an attractive picture, but it is a painting of the imagination—not a photograph of the living facts. The other method—but let us wait till we look into the days to come. . . . I have spoken of the up-and-down curves of history—or rather of the periods of quiescence followed by rushing, active progress. We are in the midst of one of the latter now. Are we at the end of it? Are we about to slow up, to begin to digest in comparative quiet the huge meal of new activities given to the human race in the past fifty years? I think not. On the contrary. I believe that more new and startling developments will take place in the immediate future than in the immediate past. With these will come other great changes in the lives and doings and thoughts of the average man and woman. Can we, by artificial means, call a halt? Obviously not." [19]

As president, Roosevelt undertook a wholehearted and thoroughgoing makeover of the nation. No more uneven progress of which he had complained a decade or so earlier. Since I,[20] and others, have written extensively about the New Deal's details, there is no purpose in rehashing them here. However, it is well summed up by Roosevelt's manifesto—his 1944 State of the Union speech, delivered near the end of his presidency, in which he proposes his Second Bill of Rights.[21]

Roosevelt told the nation, "This Republic had its beginning, and grew to its present strength, under the protection of certain inalienable political rights—among them the right of free speech, free press, free worship, trial by jury, freedom from unreasonable searches and seizures. They were our rights to life and liberty. As our nation has grown in size and stature, however—as our industrial economy expanded—these political rights proved inadequate to assure us equality in the pursuit of happiness. We have come to a clear realization of the fact that true individual freedom cannot exist without economic security and independence. Necessitous men are not free men. People who are hungry and out of a job are the stuff of which dictatorships are made."[22]

Here Roosevelt cleverly but deceptively deviated from the Declaration of Independence. Inalienable rights belong to every individual and are not political but God-given and natural. The phrase "inalienable political rights," as Roosevelt labeled them, is not unlike Wilson's use of the word *privilege*, for they both imply the government has the authority to grant or deny the individual "the right to life, liberty, and the pursuit of happiness." Therefore, the individual has no real rights independent of those recognized by the government. Furthermore, Roosevelt argued that "true individual freedom" requires "economic security." By this he did not mean the protection of the individual's private property but its antithesis—that is, the dispossession of the individual's property as the government sees fit. Of course, if individuals do not produce goods and services, there is nothing that even a mastermind can redistribute. As Locke explained, "I think it will be but a very modest computation to say, that of the products of the earth useful to the life of man, nine-tenths are the effects of labor. Nay, if we will rightly estimate things as they come to our use, and cast up the several expenses about them—what in them is purely owing to Nature and what to labor—we shall find that in most of them ninety-nine hundredths are wholly to be put on the account of labor" (5, 40). No government can re-create let alone improve upon man's nature, where he is free to invent, create, and produce; pursue, acquire, and maintain property; and enter into beneficial commercial arrangements, which not only improve the individual's life but enrich society generally.

In fact, Locke anticipated and rejected the tyranny of radical egalitarianism. "God gave the world to men in common, but since He gave it them for their benefit and the greatest conveniences of life they were capable to draw from it, it cannot be supposed He meant it should always remain common and uncultivated. He gave it to the use of the industrious and rational . . . not to the fancy or covetousness of the quarrelsome and contentious. He that has as good left for his improvement as was already taken up needed not to complain, ought not to meddle with what was already improved by another's labor. If he did, it is plain he desired the benefit of another's pains, which he had no right to, and not the ground which God had given him, in common with others, to labor on, and whereof there was as good left as that already possessed, and more than he knew what to do with, or his industry could reach to" (5, 33). Moreover, Locke argued that not only does the individual have the right to preserve his property in the state of nature, but the primary purpose of the commonwealth is to protect his property against transgressors—which is linked inextricably to "his life, liberty, and estate" (7, 87–88).

In his Second Bill of Rights, Roosevelt succinctly described the societal and economic mission to which he had committed the federal government during the course of his presidency, and which he strived to make eternal. He said, "In our day these economic truths have become accepted as self-evident. We have accepted, so to speak, a second Bill of Rights under which a new basis of security and prosperity can be established for all—regardless of station, race, or creed. Among these are: The right to a useful and remunerative job in the industries or shops or farms or mines of the nation; to earn enough to provide adequate food and clothing and recreation; of every farmer to raise and sell his products at a return which will give him and his family a decent living; of every businessman, large and small, to trade in an atmosphere of freedom from unfair competition and domination by monopolies at home or abroad; of every family to a decent home; to adequate medical care and the opportunity to achieve and enjoy good health; to adequate protection from the economic fears of old age, sickness, accident, and unemployment; to a good education." [23]

These are not rights. These are tyranny's disguise. By dominating the individual's property, the utopian dominates the individual's labor; by dominating the individual's labor, he dominates the individual. There is little space between Roosevelt's premise and the distorted historical views of Marx and Engels. They insisted that "[t]he selfish misconception that induces you to transform into eternal laws of nature and of reason, the social forms springing from your present mode of production and form of property—

historical relations that rise and disappear in the progress of production—the misconception you share with every ruling class that has preceded you. What you see clearly in the case of ancient property, what you admit in the case of feudal property, you are of course forbidden to admit in the case of your bourgeois form of property" (*The Communist Manifesto*, 39). They insisted that all ties must be severed with the past. "In bourgeois society . . . the past dominates the present; in Communist society, the present dominates the past. . . . [I]n Communist society accumulated labor is but a means to widen, to enrich, to promote the existence of the laborer" (36).

Indeed, Roosevelt's worldview harks back to Thomas More's *Utopia*, a precursor to Marx's workers' paradise, where the individual's labor and property are ultimately possessions of the masterminds and subject to their egalitarian designs. More wrote, "Thither the works of every family be brought into houses, and every kind of thing is laid up several in barns or storehouses. From hence the father of every family or every householder fetcheth whatsoever he and his have need of, and carrieth it away with him without money, without exchange, without gage, pawn, or pledge. For why should any thing be denied unto him, seeing there is abundance of all things and that it is not to be feared lest any man will ask more than he needeth? For why should it be thought that that man would ask more than enough, which is sure never to lack?" (78) And, of course, by ensuring that life's necessities are plentiful, *Utopia* eliminates poverty, inequality, and want. "This fashion and trade of life being used among the people, it cannot be chosen but they must of necessity have store and plenty of all things. And seeing they be all thereof partners equally, therefore, can no man there be poor or needy" (84).

There is no denying Roosevelt's revolutionary fervor. Whereas the Founders broke from tyranny, Roosevelt and the utopians broke from the Founders. Cass Sunstein, a former academic now employed by President Barack Obama as administrator of the Office of Information and Regulatory Affairs in the Office of Management and Budget, in 2004 wrote approvingly that "America's public institutions were radically transformed under Roosevelt's leadership. The federal government assumed powers formerly believed to rest with the states. The presidency grew dramatically in stature and importance; it became the principal seat of American democracy. A newly developed bureaucracy, including independent regulatory commissions, was put in place. The foundations of the transformation are best captured in a changing understanding of rights, often requiring helping hands. . . . By 1944, Roosevelt argued, the real task was to implement the second bill [of rights]. . . ."[24] Sunstein proclaimed, "We live under Roosevelt's Constitution whether we know it or not. The American Constitution has become, in crucial respects, his own."[25]

Roosevelt's Constitution, as Sunstein labeled it, is eerily similar in certain significant respects to the former Soviet Union's list of Fundamental Rights, set forth in Chapter X of its 1936 Constitution. For example:

ARTICLE 118. Citizens of the U.S.S.R. have the *right to work*, that is, are guaranteed the right to employment and payment for their work in accordance with its quantity and quality. . . .

ARTICLE 119. Citizens of the U.S.S.R. have the *right to rest and leisure*. . . . The institution of annual vacations with full pay for workers and employees and the provision of a wide network of sanatoria, rest homes and clubs for the accommodation of the working people.

ARTICLE 120. Citizens of the U.S.S.R. have the *right to* maintenance in old age and also in case of sickness or loss of capacity to work. This right is ensured by the *extensive development of social insurance* of workers and employees at state expense, free medical service for the working people and the provision of a wide network of health resorts for the use of the working people.

ARTICLE 121. Citizens of the U.S.S.R. have the *right to education*. This right is ensured by universal, compulsory elementary education; by education, including higher education, being free of charge; by the system of state stipends for the overwhelming majority of students in the universities and colleges. . . .[26]

What are we to make of this? Whittaker Chambers, who had been a member of the Communist Party USA, Soviet spy, proponent of the New Deal, editor at *Time* magazine, and who later condemned communism and the New Deal, wrote in his 1952 autobiography, *Witness*, "I had to acknowledge the truth of what its more forthright protagonists, sometimes unwarily, sometimes defiantly, averred: the New Deal was a genuine revolution, whose deepest purpose was not simply reform within existing traditions, but a basic change in the social and, above all, the power relationships within the nation. It was not a revolution of violence. It was a revolution by bookkeeping and lawmaking. Insofar as it was successful, the power of politics had replaced business. This is the basic power shift of all the revolutions of our time. This shift was the revolution. It was only of incidental interest that the revolution was not complete, that it was made not by tanks and machine guns, but by acts of Congress and decisions of the Supreme Court, or that many of the revolutionists did not know what they were or denied it. But revolution is always an affair of force, whatever forms the force disguises itself in. Whether the revolutionists prefer to call themselves Fabians, who seek power by the inevitability of gradualism, or Bolsheviks, who seek power by the dictatorship of the proletariat, the struggle is for power."[27]

The "living Constitution" is a constitution on its deathbed. The Founders are dismissed as quaint or worse—ancients, slaveholders, and landed gentry. This is as it must be, for utopianism is bigger than history and politics. It is a break from the past. The utopians are impatient, anxious, and frenetic, for life is short, destiny calls, and a fantastic future awaits humankind if only man, with all his flaws and imperfections, would relent or get out of the way. Therefore, the earthly grind of societal reinvention must continue unabated. One hundred years after the publication of Wilson's *Constitutional Government in the United States* and sixty-four years after Roosevelt delivered his Second Bill of Rights speech, presidential candidate Barack Obama declared, "We are five days away from fundamentally transforming the United States of America." Five days later, he was elected president.[28] The counterrevolution, which is over a century old, proceeds more thoroughly and aggressively today than before.

CHAPTER TWELVE

AMERITOPIA

It bears emphasizing — the utopian mastermind seeks control over the individual. The individual is to be governed, not represented. His personal interests are of no interest. They are dismissed as selfish, unjust, and destructive. Societal deconstruction and transformation are not possible if tens of millions of individuals are free to live their lives and pursue their interests without constant torment, coercion, and if necessary, repression. In America, breaking from the past means breaking the individual's spirit. He must be made to bend to the demands of the masterminds. He must be reshaped to serve the greater good.

There are those who are hypnotized by the utopian message, which sounds much like Karl Marx's false historicism of the material dialectic—that is, of the two-class society, where the rich bourgeois capitalists victimize the hardworking proletariat laborers, with the latter eventually destroying the former, thereby setting the stage for the end of human struggle. This kind of class warfare, pitting straw men against straw men, is now a routine and regular part of the American political dialogue. Yet, in practice, for the utopian it is better that all be poor than some be wealthy; that all suffocate from laws and regulations than some breathe free. But equality of this sort—of behavioral conformity and equivalent economic outcomes—is not the natural state of man. It is not America's history. From the first settlers to today's immigrants, America has rightly been considered exceptional—the land of individual opportunity, not the land of haves and have-nots. In America, the wealthy can fall and do, and the poor can rise and do. There is no bourgeois-versus-proletariat standoff but, instead, an immense prosperity born of an open society and economic market system that know no class structure. However, the false utopianism of radical egalitarianism incites jealousy among some if not many, divides and distracts the people, and furthers the prospects of mastermind control by changing the society's psychology and national character.

There are also those who delusively if not enthusiastically surrender their liberty for the mastermind's false promises of human and societal perfectibility. He hooks them with financial bribes in the form of "entitlements." And he makes incredible claims about indefectible health, safety, educational, and environmental policies, the success of which is to be measured not in the here and now but in the distant future.

For these reasons and more, some become fanatics for the cause. They take to the streets and, ironically, demand their own demise as they protest against their own self-determination and for ever more autocracy and authoritarianism. When they vote, they vote to enchain not only their fellow citizens but, unwittingly, themselves. Paradoxically, as the utopia metastasizes and the society ossifies, elections become less relevant. More and more decisions are made by masterminds and their experts, who substitute their self-serving and dogmatic judgments—which are proclaimed righteous and compassionate—for the individual's self-interests and best interests.

These masterminds—the politicians, judges, and bureaucrats— have become America's version of Plato's philosopher-kings and guardians, with obvious exceptions. As Plato wrote in the *Republic*, "Philosophers because of the love of Forms [a perfect thing or being], become lovers of proper order in the sensible world as well. They wish to imitate the harmony of the Forms, and so in their relations with others they are loath to do anything that violates the proper order among people" (404). Moreover, only they are able to know "the Good" (the ultimate truth). They are wise and learned beyond the capabilities of the people they rule.

But from where do the masterminds acquire their superhuman qualities? Are they born with them? Do they materialize upon election or appointment to high office? The truth is that no individual or assemblies of individuals are up to the task of managing society. They never have been and they never will be. They do not know what they do not know. As Friedrich Hayek explained, "Economics has from its origins been concerned with how an extended order of human interaction comes into existence through a process of variation, winnowing and sifting far surpassing our capacity to design. . . . In our economic activities we do not know the needs which we satisfy nor the sources of things which we get. Almost all of us serve people whom we do not know, and even of whose existence we are ignorant; and we in turn constantly live on the services of other people of whom we know nothing. All this is possible because we stand in a great framework of institutions and traditions—economic, legal, and moral—into which we fit ourselves by obeying certain rules of conduct that we never made, and which we have never understood in the sense which we understand how the things that we manufacture function."[1] There is symbiosis to the civil society in which individuals participate in an intricate system of infinite voluntary economic, social, and cultural interactions that are motivated by their needs and desires within the community.

Thus central planning is not about rationality and reason. It is not about knowledge and experience. It is about illegitimately exercising power over others. It is about the deceit of moral relativism and situationalism. It is about the coercive imposition of a hopelessly impossible utopian ideal—an ideal that is complex and ambiguous; fixed and elusive; comprehensive and piecemeal; and abrupt and gradual. However, its direction is certain, steady, and one-way—tyranny, in one form or another. It requires nonstop social engineering and intervention, in matters big and small, for it concedes no failures, acknowledges no bounds, and tolerates no deviation from dogma, which is said to be futuristic, paradisiacal, and preordained.

Post-constitutional America bears the resemblance and qualities of a utopian enterprise. Its exact form and nature elude definitional precision, but its outlines are familiar enough. It shares ambitions, albeit inexactly, not only with the hierarchical caste system in Plato's *Republic*, where the politicians and judges behave increasingly as philosopher-kings, federal bureaucrats serve as guardian enforcers, and "the masses" exist to serve the greater good of the state, but also with the artificial humanism of Thomas More's *Utopia*, where labor is managed, conformity imposed, and no one goes without; the omnipresence of Thomas Hobbes's *Leviathan*, where the individual must obey the commands of the omnipotent sovereign; and the Marx-Engels class-based radical egalitarianism and its pursuit of the inevitable workers' paradise. Over the course of the last hundred years or so, the counterrevolution has achieved significant success. There is no denying that America has become more utopian in character and less republican. In fact, it is more accurate to describe modern America not as a constitutional republic, although it retains certain constitutional and republican traits, but a utopia—an *Ameritopia*. To the extent this continues, and whether or where it ends, I cannot say, for I do not know.

The Founders would be appalled at the nature of the federal government's transmutation and the squandering of the American legacy. The federal government has become the nation's largest creditor, debtor, lender, employer, consumer, contractor, grantor, property owner, tenant, insurer, health-care provider, and pension guarantor. Its size and reach are vast. Its interventions are illimitable. As I am constrained by time, space, and the human condition, it is not possible to set out an all-inclusive examination of the state of things. However, certain examples, both general in nature and common to daily life, should help prove the point to those who remain open to reason and keen on liberty. If further evidence is desired, it abounds everywhere and permeates everyday existence. One need only make the effort to observe it.

FEDERAL TAXING, SPENDING, AND DEBT

Among the ten tenets in *The Communist Manifesto*, Marx and Engels include "[a] heavy progressive or graduated income tax" (42). In America, the federal government imposes a staggering burden on a small fraction of taxpayers, as reflected in data released by the Internal Revenue Service for 2008. The top 1 percent of income earners paid 38 percent of personal income taxes while earning 20 percent of pretax income. The top 5 percent of income earners paid 58.7 percent of personal income taxes while earning 34.7 percent of pretax income. Meanwhile, the bottom 50 percent of income earners paid only 2.7 percent of the total tax burden while earning 12.75 percent of the total pretax income. In other words, the top 5 percent of income earners paid the majority of the total tax burden and the bottom half of income earners paid almost nothing.[2]

Gross domestic product (GDP) represents the total value of all goods and services produced in the United States in a given year. In 1930, the federal government spent 3.4 percent of GDP. In 1937 and 1939, in the midst of the Great Depression, federal expenditures consumed 8.6 percent and 10.3 percent of the GDP, respectively. During 1943 and 1944, in the midst of World War II, expenditures were 43.5 percent and 43.6 percent, respectively. In 1948, after the war, the percentage dropped to 11.5 percent. Throughout the 1950s and 1960s, federal expenditures as a percentage of GDP hovered between 15 percent and 17 percent. During the 1970s and 1980s, these numbers ranged between 17 percent and 19 percent. In the 1990s, the percentage varied between 15 percent and 19 percent. By 2000 and 2001, there was a small drop to 14.8 percent in both years. Starting in 2009, the percentage reached 21.1 percent—the highest percentage of federal spending since 1946.[3] And in 2010, federal expenditures jumped to 24 percent of GDP.[4]

Moreover, at the end of 2008, the federal debt as a percentage of GDP was at 40 percent.[5] In 2010, it jumped to over 60 percent.[6] For 2011, the Congressional Budget Office (CBO) projects the federal debt will reach about 70 percent of GDP, the highest level since right after World War II, and it will exceed 100 percent of GDP by 2012. Shortly thereafter, "the growing imbalance between revenues and spending, combined with spiraling interest payments, would swiftly push debt to higher and higher levels. . . ."[7]

Furthermore, the most recent estimate of total unfunded obligations in dollar terms—for which no resources are currently available and will never be available—is $61.6 trillion, or $528,000 per household.[8] This includes $25 trillion in unfunded obligations for Medicare, $21.4 trillion for Social Security, and $9.4 trillion for servicing the debt.[9]

REGULATIONS AND THE ADMINISTRATIVE STATE

Congress has established a massive administrative state that serves as an unconstitutional fourth governmental branch and exercises legislative, executive, and judicial powers. It employs an army of more than two million bureaucrats who work for an untold number of departments, agencies, bureaus, divisions, boards, etc. They are highly compensated, with average salary and benefits more than double what employees in the private sector earn.[10] Yet the administrative state operates mostly on autopilot, with minimal oversight by the constitutionally established branches of government. It monitors daily life and attempts to mechanically extinguish risk, dissimilarity, and choice, as well as that which has become routine and acceptable, in pursuit of societal perfection.

The administrative state issues thousands of regulations and rulings every year, which have the force of law. The Competitive Enterprise Institute reported that the 2010 *Federal Register*, the official compendium of federal rules, totaled 81,405 pages, a record high. Since 2001, 38,700 final regulations have been promulgated. In 2010 alone, 3,573 rules were enacted by federal agencies.[11] An evaluation by economists Nicole V. Crain and W. Mark Crain determined that private sector regulatory compliance costs amounted to $1.752 trillion in 2008, absorbing 11.9 percent of the total gross domestic product of the nation.[12] Moreover, The Heritage Foundation found that the number of criminal offenses in the United States Code increased from 3,000 in the early 1980s to 4,000 by 2000, to over 4,450 by 2008. But the total number of criminal offenses is actually unknown even to the federal government, which establishes them. "Scores of federal departments and agencies have created so many criminal offenses that the Congressional Research Service (CRS) [the research arm of Congress] . . . admitted that it was unable to even count all of the offenses. The Service's best estimate? 'Tens of thousands.' . . . Congress's own experts do not have a clear understanding of the size and scope of federal criminalization."[13]

However, even an abridged examination of the federal regulatory regime reveals the extent of its tentacles. For example, when constructing a home, federal rules set standards for insulation, gypsum board, treated lumber, windows, pipes, ventilation ducts, flooring, paint, etc. Homebuilders must comply with the Clean Air Act, the Clean Water Act, the Endangered Species Act, the Resource Conservation and Recovery Act, the Toxic Substances Control Act, and the National Historic Preservation Act.[14] If water on the property meets the Clean Water Act definition of wetland, a permit must be secured by the property owner from the Army Corps of Engineers before the wet area can be filled with dirt. The definition of wetland is broad enough to include land that is not actually a wetland, such as "those areas that are inundated or saturated by surface or groundwater at a frequency and duration sufficient to support, and that under normal circumstances do support, a prevalence of vegetation typically adapted for life in saturated soil conditions."[15]

Inside the home, the federal government regulates washing machines, dryers, dishwashers, dishwasher detergents, microwave ovens, toilets, showerheads, heating and cooling systems, refrigerators, freezers, furnace fans and boilers, ceiling fans, dehumidifiers, lightbulbs, certain renovations, fitness equipment, clothing, baby cribs, pacifiers, rattles and toys, marbles, latex balloons, matchbooks, bunk beds, mattresses, mattress pads, televisions, radios, cell phones, iPods and other digital media devices, computer components, video recording devices, speakers, batteries, battery chargers, power supplies, stereo equipment, garage door openers, lawn mowers, lawn darts, pool slides, etc. The federal government also regulates toothpaste, deodorant, dentures, and most things in and around the medicine cabinet.[16]

Like the home, so much of the automobile is regulated by the federal government. The Heartland Institute reported that federal mandates set standards for "automobiles' engines, bumpers, headrests, seat belts, door latches, brakes, fuel systems, and windshields" as well as side-door guard beams and energy-absorbing steering columns.[17] Add to this airbags, a centered/rear brake light, and electronic stability control system. Moreover, the Cato Institute reported that Corporate Average Fuel Economy (CAFE) standards require new car fleets to average 35.5 mpg by 2016. For an automobile manufacturer, it means for every 15-mpg model, five models will have to average 50 mpg.[18] The federal government is requiring that by 2025, automobile car fleets average 54.5 mpg.[19] Not only will the cost of these new standards be enormous,[20] but CAFE standards have resulted in tens of thousands more deaths and injuries, since they require vehicles to be lighter.[21]

For years the federal government mandated that automobiles be sold only with labels on their windows that displayed their fuel efficiency levels. Beginning in 2013, all new passenger cars and trucks will be required to have more extensive window labels describing: emissions of smog-forming pollution and carbon dioxide, as well as a 1–10 rating showing how a model's emission levels compared to other new vehicles; projected annual fuel costs for each vehicle; each vehicle's fuel costs over a five-year period compared to other new vehicles; projected city, highway, and combined miles-per-gallon fuel efficiency performance; a separate estimate of how many gallons will be required to fuel a vehicle for one hundred miles of travel; and labels for plug-in hybrid electric vehicles and electric vehicles, comparing pollution levels with gasoline-powered vehicles.[22] The federal government requires that the labels be "useful" and "easy-to-read."[23]

The federal government has instituted overlapping review processes and regulations, involving multiple agencies, discouraging the development of the fuel that powers the automobile.[24] Once discovered and processed, the producers or importers of gasoline, diesel fuels, or fuel additives must register their products with the federal government before introducing them into the market.[25] They must ensure that their gasoline is blended with the requisite percentages of specific types of biofuels. They are required to produce seasonal and regional variants. For renewable fuels, they must generate specific identification numbers to track their production and ensure compliance with mandated quotas.[26]

In addition to the scores of federal regulations respecting the transportation of fuel, the retail gasoline station that dispenses the fuel to the consumer is also regulated by the federal government. The "National Emission Standards for Hazardous Air Pollutants: Gasoline Dispensing Facilities" imposes requirements for seals and vapor locks and regulates underground storage tanks.[27] The retailer must also post the automotive fuel rating of all automotive fuel sold to customers. One label must be placed on each face of each dispenser through which automotive fuel is sold. If the retailer does not blend the gasoline with other gasoline, he must post the octane rating of the gasoline consistent with the octane rating certified to him by the dealer. If the gasoline is blended with other gasoline, he must post the rating consistent with his determination of the average, weighted by volume, of the octane ratings certified to him for each gasoline in the blend, or consistent with the lowest octane rating certified to him for any gasoline in the blend. In cases involving gasoline, the octane rating must be shown as a whole or half number equal to or less than the number certified to the retailer or determined by him. If he does not blend alternative liquid automotive fuels, he must post consistent with the automotive fuel rating certified to him. If he blended alternative liquid automotive fuels, he must possess a reasonable basis, consisting of competent and reliable evidence, for the automotive fuel rating he posts for the blend.[28]

Incidentally, that cinnamon doughnut the gasoline retailer sells in the snack food section of his store is supplied by a bakery that must comply with federal regulations requiring that all pulverizing of sugar or spice grinding be done in accordance with sugar dust limitation standards.[29] Of course, there are all kinds of regulations that apply to virtually all other food items he stocks on his shelves.

Indeed, not just food, but food labeling and packaging are subject to extensive federal regulation. New mandates require food labels "to disclose net contents, identity of commodity, and name and place of business of the product's manufacturer, packer, or distributor." Labels must also include the presence of major food allergens. Certain terms like "low sodium," "reduced fat," and "high fiber" must meet strict government definitions. The federal government has defined other terms used for nutritional content including "low," "reduced," "high," "free," "lean," "extra lean," "good source," "less," and "lite." If a food is described as "organic" it must meet the federal government's definition.[30] The food industry will also face new federal rules for "front-of-pack" calorie and nutrition labels and federally recommended nutritional criteria for foods making "dietary guidance" statements. For example, "Eat two cups of fruit a day for good health." Federal regulations also involve "food contact materials," including cutlery, dishes, glasses, cups, food processors, containers, etc.[31]

The administrative state is also foster-parenting the nation's children. Aiming their regulatory power at such foods as Frosted Flakes, the Food and Drug Administration, Centers for Disease Control and Prevention, United States Department of Agriculture, and Federal Trade Commission recently joined forces to propose "voluntary" nutrition principles for the food industry, including setting limits on sugar, fats, and sodium in food marketed to children. "By the year 2016, all food products within the categories most heavily marketed directly to children should meet two basic nutrition principles. Such foods should be formulated to . . . make a meaningful contribution to a healthful diet and minimize the content of nutrients that could have a negative impact on health and weight."[32] The Working Group's proposals go beyond cereal and would affect snacks, candy, juice, soda, and even food served at restaurants. In addition to restricting the content of food, the Working Group is also entertaining proposals to regulate what can be included in product advertising.[33] Tony the Tiger may be on the chopping block. Congress also passed legislation authorizing the administrative state to regulate nutrition in schools, including determining the amount of calories, fat, and sodium students should consume each day. The regulations may extend to food sold on school grounds during the day, such as pizza and bake sales at fund-raisers for school events, potentially ending those common practices.[34]

Restaurants have been hectored into accepting the "goals of smaller portions" to "include healthy offerings" in children's meals.[35] Federal requirements mandate that restaurant chains with at least twenty U.S. locations provide the calorie content of menu items. Chain restaurants are obligated to adhere to a host of requirements pertaining to the listing of food items on their menus, including "[a] statement on the menu or menu board that puts the calorie information in the context of a recommended total daily caloric intake."[36] Federal regulators are expanding the restaurant requirements to movie theater concessions, which will soon be compelled to disclose the calorie information for popcorn.[37]

So extensive is the federal government's purview over food that the total federal budget for regulating nearly all aspects of food, from production to consumption, exceeds the entire country's net farm income.[38]

The workplace is subject to a web of federal regulations. Where "public accommodation" is involved, such as a retail store or doctor's office, there must be ramps, special bathrooms, widened doors, and curb cuts in the sidewalks. Even carpeting is scrutinized to make sure it is accessible.[39] There are rules involving wages, taxes, health benefits, pension benefits, working conditions, environmental conditions, human resources, union elections, financial practices, and record keeping. The vending machine on the premises is regulated. It must have a "sign close to each article of food or selection button disclosing the amount of calories in a clear and conspicuous manner."[40]

As I said earlier, the universe of federal regulations and their interpretations are too far-reaching and wide-ranging to catalogue and decipher here. Indeed, left unsaid are federal rules aimed at regulating so-called man-made global warming and carbon dioxide, which would engulf the private sector in one grand sweep; and the federal directives and mandates involving education at all levels, including instruction, funding, etc. Instead, these relatively few examples are intended to provide perspective and make tangible the extent to which the individual lives under increasingly burdensome controls imposed by a federal government that determines its own authority. Private interests, including property rights, are of little regard and nearly impossible to safeguard. Moreover, private citizens on whom the government imposes the duty to institute federal regulations are overwhelmed by the coercive powers of the administrative state, including audits, fines, penalties, confiscation of licenses and property, and prosecution. The hugely detrimental effects on human progress—including preventing, sabotaging, and discouraging the development of new lifesaving and life-improving technologies, processes, and products; wealth and job creation; and individual industriousness and self-sufficiency—are fatal to societal vitality.

There are those who blindly accept if not demand federal intrusion whenever and wherever it is said to improve "health, safety, education, and the environment." For them, it is enough for the masterminds and their experts to claim their intention to improve man's condition. These individuals, it seems, are the type of citizens More had in mind in *Utopia*, where the Prince "will declare how the citizens use themselves one towards another; what familiar occupying and entertainment there is among the people; and what fashion they use in the distribution of every thing" (76). However, even in the smothering atmosphere of *Leviathan*, where the liberty of the subject (the citizen) is regulated by the all-powerful sovereign, Hobbes acknowledged its practical limits. "For seeing there is no commonwealth in the world wherein there be rules enough set down for the regulating of all kinds of actions and words of men (as being a thing impossible), it followeth necessarily that in all kinds of actions by the laws praetermitted, men have the liberty of doing what their own reasons shall suggest for the most profitable of themselves. . . ." (138) But do they? It is the endless pursuit of the utopian abstraction that tyrannizes the individual and society. As Charles de Montesquieu observed, "Countries which have been made inhabitable by the industry of men and which need that same industry in order to exist call for moderate government" (43, 18, 6).

How did we Americans cope before the advent of such a massive and intrusive administrative state? How did we feed, clothe, transport, and house ourselves? How did we make decisions about our health, safety, and well-being, and consumer items large and small? How did we raise our children and educate them, and manage our finances and retirement?

During his travels in America, Alexis de Tocqueville marveled that "[t]he secondary affairs of society have never been regulated by [the central government's] authority; and nothing has hitherto betrayed its desire of even interfering in them. . . ." (I, 271) He observed that if such decrees were ordered, the federal government "must entrust the execution of its will to agents over whom it frequently has no control and who it cannot perpetually direct. The townships, municipal bodies, and counties form so many concealed breakwaters. . . ." (I, 272) Yet he foretold democracy's vulnerability to administrative despotism, although he had hoped America would avoid its infliction because of its unique history and circumstances. "Above this race of men stands an intense and tutelary power, which takes upon itself alone to secure their gratifications and to watch over their fate. That power is absolute, minute, regular, provident, and mild. It would be like the authority of a parent if, like that authority, its object was to prepare men for manhood; but it seeks, on the contrary, to keep them in perpetual childhood . . . it every day renders the exercise of free agency of man less useful and less frequent; it circumscribes the will within a narrower range and gradually robs a man of all his uses of himself. . . . It covers the surface of society with a network of small complicated rules, minute and uniform, through which the most original minds and the most energetic characters cannot penetrate, to rise above the crowd. . . ." "Such a power . . . compresses, enervates, extinguishes, and stupefies a people" who are "reduced to nothing better than a flock of timid and industrious animals, of which the government is the shepherd" (I, 318–19).

America has become a society in which the people are wise enough to select their own leaders, but too incompetent to choose the right lightbulb.

"ENTITLEMENTS" AND THE ADMINISTRATIVE STATE

Another aspect of the administrative state involves so-called entitlements. In the United States, the concept of "social insurance" can be traced back to the work of Columbia University professor Henry Rogers Seager. In his 1910 work, *Social Insurance: A Program of Social Reform*,[41] Seager provided a framework for Social Security, among other government social programs. In turn, Seager was heavily influenced by European models of socialism.[42]

Seager constantly attacked the American "absorption" with individualism as he promoted Europe's "cooperative movement."[43] "As though it were not enough that heredity and environment combined to make us individualists, our forefathers wrote their individualistic creed into our federal and state constitutions. All these instruments give special sanctity to the rights to liberty and property. . . . Thus it is not too much to say that Americans are born individualists in a country peculiarly favorable to the real-ization of individual ambitions and under a legal system which discourages and opposes resort to any but individualistic remedies for social evils."[44] He added that in those areas of the nation in-volved in manufacturing and trade "we need not freedom from government interference, but clear appreciation of the conditions that make for the common welfare, as contrasted with individual success, and an aggressive program of governmental control and regulation to maintain these conditions."[45]

Seager proceeded to lay out the general terms of what would become the Social Security program. He argued, "The proper method of safeguarding old age is clearly through some plan of insurance. . . . The intelligent course is for [the wage earner] to combine with other wage earners to accumulate a common fund out of which old-age annuities may be paid to those who live long enough to need them."[46] Seager praised the insurance programs of certain large corporations and foreign countries, particularly in the United Kingdom and Germany. He believed that the best aspects of these systems should be adopted by the federal govern-ment and turned into compulsory old-age insurance. This would require "vigorous government action."[47] But given the resistance to this and other social programs in the United States at the time, because of the history of individualism and its federal form of gov-ernment, there must be "political reform" and "industrial educa-tion"[48] to develop a "deepening of the sense of social solidarity and quickening of appreciation of our common interests," both of which are "indispensable to the realization of any program of so-cial reform."[49] "Only by a change of attitude and change of heart on the part of the whole people can we hope to curb our rampant individualism and achieve those common ends which we all admit to be desirable but which are only attainable through our united efforts. As soon as we begin to think of government as something more than an agency for maintaining order,—as organized machinery for advancing our common interests,—we appreciate how far we still are from being a truly civilized society."[50] Hence there must be a counterrevolution in which the psychology of the American people and the nature of their government are radically transformed.

Again and again, Seager targeted what he considered the greatest obstacle to "social reform"—individualism. "The gospel of love has as yet influenced very little our views on public questions. In business and in politics we are still individualists. We habitually put our individual before our common interests, and even when we are conscious of common needs we hesitate to intrust them to our common government. To correct these national characteristics is . . . the most important next step in social advance. And as we correct them, as our sense of social solidarity is deepened, and our appreciation of our common interests quickened, measures of reform will seem obvious and easy that now seem visionary and impracticable."[51] "Let us not be frightened by phrases, by the bugaboo of 'destroying local self-government,' . . . of 'undermining individual thrift,' or of 'socialism.' This is the truly scientific attitude toward a field of phenomena where all is change and development."[52] Seager makes no effort to conceal his attack on the nature and spirit of the individual. Importantly, Seager's views were influential on President Franklin Roosevelt and his brain trust.

In her book *Dependent on D.C.*, Professor Charlotte A. Twight

explained how Social Security was decisive in promoting the psychological and political transformation of the nation. She wrote,
"Contrary to conventional wisdom, the public did not desire
the compulsory old-age 'insurance' program that we call Social
Security. . . . It was passed [in 1935] and later expanded despite
initial public opposition and strongly prevailing ideologies of self-
reliance. Social Security's history unfolded as a montage of political transaction-cost manipulation that included governmental
use of insurance imagery, incrementalism, cost concealment, information control and censorship, suppression of rival programs,
and a myth of actuarial balance. Its primary targets were the program's congressional opponents and, especially, the voting public. In the end, these strategies moved Social Security from being
regarded as a dangerous socialistic invasion of American life to
an almost sacrosanct institution." [53] In fact, "as late as 1934, five
years into the Depression, 'a bill had not yet been introduced into
Congress for compulsory old-age insurance' because 'there were
simply no significant demands for such a program.' Even after the
administration's proposal was introduced, 'no groundswell developed in support of social insurance programs because they did
not affect the major problems of relieving the victims of the depression.' Depression conditions did stimulate public sentiment
favoring needs-based (that is, means-tested) public assistance for
the aged poor, but President Roosevelt instead sought a broader
'contributory' program of compulsory old-age insurance. When a
widely supported bill to provide needs-based public assistance for
the elderly neared passage in 1934, Roosevelt strategically urged
its deferral. . . ." [54]

It serves the purposes of the utopian masterminds to enlist or ensnare as many people as possible in their cause. The objective is to cut generational ties with the past—society's traditions, customs, and beliefs—in order to transform and restructure society. The common psychology that brought individuals together in the first place, making them "the American people," must be suppressed and reoriented. The people must be reeducated and indoctrinated to accept utopian dictates, or as the utopians call them, "social reforms."

Programs such as Social Security and Medicare serve the utopian purpose, for they create a widespread dependency on a post-constitutional government and its masterminds. These schemes are built on the illusion that the individual has a vested ownership interest in, for example, a pension or insurance program. Through forced taxation, misleadingly referred to as "contributions," the individual is encouraged to believe that he has, in effect, purchased a pension annuity or health insurance policy, which becomes his personal property. But his tax dollars are actually subsidizing others, and later others will subsidize his retirement and medical care in what is an elaborate and unsustainable undertaking. As such, it falls on future generations, including children and grandchildren yet born, to sort out the financial ruin and societal havoc let loose by the masterminds.

Roosevelt understood, and intended, that individuals would rely on these misrepresentations and false promises and plan their retirements around them. After all, the hoax goes so far as to require that pay stubs show the funds deducted from every paycheck, which are then tracked by the federal government to presumably fund the individual's personal retirement and medical benefits. Individuals logically conclude that they have a "right" or "entitlement" to the benefits for which they paid over a lifetime of work. Any attempt to alter the conditions and benefits in this arrangement is seen by the individual as a violation of his property rights and an injustice. For the mastermind, it is an exploitable opportunity to ingratiate himself with the "masses" as he positions himself as the defender of those rights. That said, the mastermind frequently alters the arrangement, including in small ways that are difficult for the individual to discern, or in bigger ways that are masked with self-serving declarations and cloaked in deceit. But the basic structure must never change, for the utopian must never relinquish control.

As Roosevelt himself explained when criticized that the Social Security payroll tax was regressive, "Those [Social Security payroll] taxes were never a problem of economics. They are politics all the way through. We put those payroll taxes there so as to give the contributors a legal, moral, and political right to collect their pensions and their unemployment benefits. With those taxes in there, no damn politician can ever scrap my social security program."[55] By this Roosevelt meant that the utopian pursuit is an undying pursuit.

In 1966, Social Security Administration official John Carroll put it this way: "It can scarcely be contested that earmarking of payroll taxes . . . reduced resistance to the imposition of taxes on low-income earners, made feasible tax increases at a time when they might not otherwise have been made, and has given trust fund programs a privileged position semi-detached from the remainder of government. Institutionalists foresaw these advantages as means to graft the new programs into the social fabric."[56]

Social Security is the single biggest program in the federal government. In 2010, it paid benefits to almost 54 million individuals.[57]

So successful was the Social Security deception that in 1965, President Lyndon Johnson used it as the basis for establishing Medicare and Medicaid. As Twight noted, it is not widely remembered that in 1960, Congress had already passed the Kerr-Mills bill—a needs-based medical program to assist the aged poor.[58] But a welfare program instituted exclusively to subsidize medical care for poor patients cannot be convincingly presented as an insurance program. Nor can it engulf enough individuals in the utopian cause.

Johnson insisted on a new entitlement that would cover nearly all individuals age sixty-five and older. The opportunity arose in 1964 with the Democratic Party's landslide victory. When he signed the Medicare bill, Johnson said, "In 1935, when . . . Franklin Delano Roosevelt signed the Social Security Act, he said it was, and I quote him, 'a cornerstone in a structure which is being built but it is by no means complete.' . . . And those who share this day will also be remembered for making the most important addition to that structure. . . ."[59] Johnson added, "Through this new law . . . every citizen will be able, in his productive years when he is earning, to insure himself against the ravages of illness in his old age. . . ."[60] Like Roosevelt, Johnson understood the import of misleading the American people by packaging Medicare's taxes and costs as insurance and dissembling about its economic viability. As Wilbur Mills, the chairman of the House Ways and Means Committee, told Johnson when informing him that his committee had passed the Medicare bill, "I think we've got you something that we won't only run on in '66 but we'll run on from here after."[61] In 2010, Medicare covered 38.7 million people over age sixty-five and 7.6 million people with disabilities.[62]

Again, in 2010, the CBO estimated that unfunded obligations for Medicare and Social Security are $25 *trillion* and $21.4 *trillion*, respectively.[63] Both programs are economically unviable.

An analysis by the Peter G. Peterson Foundation of the 2011 Social Security Trustees' financial report found that Social Security is in a weakened financial position in the short run and in an unsustainable condition in the long run. "Social Security is now operating with a permanent, annual cash flow deficit. Within seven years, the Trustees estimate that Social Security will not be able to pay full disability benefits scheduled under current law. The Disability Insurance program will begin running permanent cash deficits. Its trust fund will be exhausted in 2018. Absent reform, Social Security will only be able to pay approximately 77 percent of scheduled benefits under current law after 2036. After this date, the program will only have the legal authority to pay benefits equal to the amount of revenue generated by the payroll tax and the taxation of some benefits."[64]

The chief actuary for Medicare, Richard S. Foster, stated that the shortfalls facing Medicare are even worse than reported by the Medicare trustees. He wrote that "the financial projections shown in [the 2011 trustees' report] do not represent a reasonable expectation for actual program operations."[65] The trustees had reported that Medicare will be unable to meet its obligations starting in 2024.[66]

The economic impossibility of these programs was never a utopian concern. Although cost-cutting, price controls, and benefit denials are instituted haphazardly, there can be no retreat from the overall mission and the centralized control and planning of the masterminds. Instead, further consolidation is nearly always the answer. Centralized control over health-care decisions in particular has been a utopian priority from the earliest for it maximizes government authority over the individual. In the *Republic*, only those who were otherwise healthy, but suffered either an injury or seasonal malady, were entitled to medical care. Those who were chronically ill, old, or infirm were of no benefit to the Ideal City and denied treatment (407d, 406b–c). In *Utopia*, magnificent hospitals were located near each city. "These hospitals be so well appointed, and with all things necessary to health so furnished . . . there is no sick person in all the city that had not rather lie there than at home in his house" (79). However, those who suffered from incurable diseases or fatal conditions were urged to kill themselves to alleviate their pain and their burden on society (107).

In America, for more than one hundred years, the utopians have insisted on the institution of government-run universal health care, promoting it in egalitarian terms. It was among the "rights" listed in Roosevelt's Second Bill of Rights. Every person, he argued, has "the right to adequate medical care and the opportunity to achieve and enjoy good health."[67] In his 1948 State of the Union speech, President Harry Truman asserted, "The greatest gap in our social security structure is the lack of adequate provision for the Nation's health. . . . I have often and strongly urged that this condition demands a national health program. The heart of the program must be a national system of payment for medical care based on well-tried insurance principles. . . . Our ultimate aim must be a comprehensive insurance system to protect all our people equally against insecurity and ill health."[68] Proclamations and proposals of this kind have littered the political landscape, and successful legislative efforts have moved America piecemeal in this direction.

However, in 2009, with Barack Obama as president and a supermajority Democratic Congress, the utopian counterrevolution reached a new pinnacle, for there were no legislative obstacles and few remaining constitutional impediments to stop or even slow its advance. The utopians seized the opportunity they had long craved to centralize and consolidate control over the entire health-care system. Late on March 22, 2010, despite much arm-twisting, deal-making, and secret negotiating, the Democratic-controlled House barely passed the nearly three-thousand-page-long "Patient Protection and Affordable Care Act" (PPACA) by a margin of 219 to 212. As with the initial adoption of Social Security and Medicare, there was no great clamor for the PPACA when it was adopted. Indeed, it was opposed by the public. A few days before its passage, Gallup found that "more Americans believe the new legislation will make things worse rather than better for the U.S. as a whole, as well as for them personally," and its latest poll was "consistent with previous Gallup polls showing a slight negative tilt when Americans are asked if they support the new plan."[69]

Most in Congress who voted for the bill had not read it, not only because of its length and complexity, but because the final version had not been made available to them, or the public, until shortly before it was voted on in the House. As intended, its concealment prevented critical scrutiny of its particulars. As then-Speaker Nancy Pelosi, just a few weeks prior to the vote, told the Legislative Conference for the National Association of Counties, "We have to pass the bill so that you can find out what is in it. . . ."[70]

In a letter to his close friend James Madison after the Constitutional Convention adopted the Constitution and sent it to the states for ratification, Thomas Jefferson warned of the diabolical nature of this kind of legislating, which has as its purpose to keep both the diligent representative and the citizen in the dark. He told Madison, "The instability of our laws is really an immense evil. I think it would be well to provide in our constitutions that there shall always be a twelvemonth between the ingrossing a bill and passing it: that it should then be offered to its passage without changing a word; and that if circumstances should be thought to require a speedier passage, it should take two thirds of both houses instead of a bare majority." [71]

But the particulars were less important to the utopian lawmakers and the president than the universality of the law. Its size and reach, in all its iterations, were known to be enormous. As former president Bill Clinton insisted, "It's not important to be perfect here. It's important to act, to move, to start the ball rolling. There will be amendments to this effort, whatever they pass, next year and the year after and the year after, and there should be. It's a big, complicated, organic thing. But the worst thing to do is nothing." [72] In other words, it was important to exploit the recent election to diminish the outcome of the next one, should it be lost to the opposition, and install a universal health-care scheme as quickly as possible. It was left to favored "experts" and special-interest third parties to work out most of the details. The routine is a familiar one: temporary politicians establishing permanent societal changes by using the law to seize the individual's sovereignty and transfer control over it to the administrative state.

Meanwhile, like Roosevelt and Johnson, Obama used deception and manipulation in hopes of rallying popular support from the very individuals whose sovereignty he sought to control. During the health-care debate, Obama claimed that "no matter how we reform health care, we will keep this promise to the American people: if you like your doctor, you will be able to keep your doctor, period. If you like your health care plan, you'll be able to keep your health care plan, period. No one will take it away, no matter what."[73] However, McKinsey and Company's "early-2011 survey of more than 1,300 employers across industries, geographies, and employer sizes, as well as other proprietary research, found that . . . 30 percent of employers will definitely or probably stop offering [health care] in the years after 2014," once the PPACA has been fully implemented.[74]

Obama insisted that "the underlying argument . . . has to be addressed, and that is people's concern that if we are reforming the health care system to make it more efficient, which I think we have to do, the concern is that somehow that will mean rationing of care, right? That somehow some government bureaucrat out there saying, well, you can't have this test or you can't have this procedure because some bean-counter decides that is not a good way to use health care dollars. . . ."[75] He went on, "So, I just want to be very clear about this. . . . You will have not only the care you need, but also the care that right now is being denied to you [by insurance companies]—only if we get health care reform."[76] But Professor Martin Feldstein pointed out at the time that "[a]lthough administration officials are eager to deny it, rationing health care is central . . . to Obama's health plan. The Obama strategy is to reduce health costs by rationing the services that we and future generations of patients will receive. The White House Council of Economic Advisers issued a report in June explaining the Obama administration's goal of reducing projected health spending by 30% over the next two decades. That reduction would be achieved by eliminating 'high cost, low-value treatments,' by 'implementing a set of performance measures that all providers would adopt,' and by 'directly targeting individual providers . . . (and other) high-end outliers.' "[77]

Obama argued that health-care reform "will slow the growth of health care costs for our families, our businesses, and our government." He declared, "I will not sign a plan that adds one dime to our deficit, now or in the future, period." However, Hewitt Associates and Mercer both reported that the PPACA was contributing to premium hikes;[78] the Congressional Budget Office disclosed that it will cost 800,000 jobs;[79] it reported further that the program will likely cost $115 billion more than originally estimated;[80] and the secretary of Health and Human Services admitted that $500 billion in supposed savings resulted from double-counting funds cut from the Medicare program.[81]

Plato, in the *Republic*, would have approved of Obama's mendacity, as he would have approved of Roosevelt's and Johnson's earlier. "The noble lie," as Plato called it, conditioned citizens to surrender their personal desires and happiness to the needs of the City and the common good. He wrote that it also promotes patriotism and eliminates political factionalism (415d). Of course, there is nothing noble about it. Obama knew full well that his pronouncements were distortions. Former Harvard University professor Donald Berwick explained in 2008 that "[a]ny health care funding plan that is just, equitable, civilized, and humane must, must redistribute wealth from the richer among us to the poorer and less fortunate. Excellent health care is by definition redistributionist."[82] Obama demonstrated his agreement with Berwick's sentiment when, in 2010, he appointed Berwick to oversee the federal government's massive Medicare and Medicaid programs.

As Obama said in 2008, "When you spread the wealth around, it's good for everybody."[83]

However, more than a year after its passage, and before 2014, when its most onerous provisions kick in, the PPACA remains unpopular with the American people.[84] But rather than be deterred, the utopian masterminds are moving fast to institutionalize the law in the administrative state, making it much more difficult to disentangle should they lose control of the elected branches in subsequent election cycles. More than $100 billion was secreted into the bill to fund its start-up, bypassing the usual congressional appropriations process.[85]

An analysis by Peter Ferrara of the Heartland Institute revealed that the PPACA establishes more than "150 new bureaucracies, agencies, boards, commissions and programs" that "are empowered to tell doctors and hospitals what is quality health care and what is not, what are best practices in medicine, how their medical practices should be structured, and what they will be paid and when."[86] The Congressional Research Service reported, "The precise number of new entities that will ultimately be created pursuant to PPACA is currently unknowable."[87] Consequently, oversight will be practically impossible and the health-care system, and particularly the individual patient, will be overwhelmed by an administrative monstrosity. What is certain is that the individual will lose control over his own health-care decisions—his physical well-being and survival—since the purpose of the PPACA is to centralize health-care decision-making over all of society.

Yet the most pernicious aspect of the PPACA has nothing to do with health care per se. Specifically, the statute dictates that an individual who does not have health insurance but who can afford it must purchase a private health insurance policy, whether he wants to or not, or face federal fines and penalties.[88] In response to litigation challenging the constitutionality of this "individual mandate," the Obama administration argues that the mandate is nothing more than Congress exercising its authority under the Constitution's Commerce Clause. However, the Commerce Clause provides, "The Congress shall have Power . . . To regulate Commerce with Foreign Nations, and among the several States, and with the Indian Tribes."[89] The plain meaning of this language provides no support for the authority the federal government demands. Congress can tax interstate commerce, regulate interstate commerce, and even prohibit certain types of interstate commerce. But there is nothing in the history of the nation, let alone the history of the Constitution and the Commerce Clause, empowering Congress or any part of the federal government to regulate inactivity and compel an individual to enter into commerce—that is, to enter into a legally binding private contract against the individual's will and interests simply because the individual is living and breathing.

Should such a specious and brazen contortion of fact and history prevail in the courts as a constitutionally recognized and legally enforceable imperative, the contours of utopian society and the mastermind's authority would seem unconfined. Thereafter, the individual's free will ceases to be free or his will. The mastermind's duping becomes an unnecessary artifice, for the federal government can now flatly dictate the individual's behavior, and the individual is without lawful recourse. Tyranny, then, will reveal itself, unvarnished and unequivocal, with future governmental trespasses on individual sovereignty both certain and more onerous.

EPILOGUE

MY PREMISE, IN THE first sentence of the first chapter of this book, is this: "Tyranny, broadly defined, is the use of power to dehumanize the individual and delegitimize his nature. Political utopianism is tyranny disguised as a desirable, workable, and even paradisiacal governing ideology."

Plato's *Republic*, More's *Utopia*, Hobbes's *Leviathan*, and Marx's workers' paradise are utopias that are anti-individual and anti-individualism. For the utopians, modern and olden, the individual is one-dimensional—selfish. On his own, he has little moral value. Contrarily, authoritarianism is defended as altruistic and masterminds as socially conscious. Thus endless interventions in the individual's life and manipulation of his conditions are justified as not only necessary and desirable but noble governmental pursuits. This false dialectic is at the heart of the problem we face today.

In truth, man is naturally independent and self-reliant, which are attributes that contribute to his own well-being and survival, and the well-being and survival of a civil society. He is also a social being who is charitable and compassionate. History abounds with examples, as do the daily lives of individuals. To condemn individualism as the utopians do is to condemn the very foundation of the civil society and the American founding and endorse, wittingly or unwittingly, oppression. Karl Popper saw it as an attack on Western civilization. "The emancipation of the individual was indeed the great spiritual revolution which had led to the breakdown of tribalism and to the rise of democracy."[1] Moreover, Judaism and Christianity, among other religions, teach the altruism of the individual.

Of course, this is not to defend anarchy. Quite the opposite. It is to endorse the magnificence of the American founding. The American founding was an exceptional exercise in collective human virtue and wisdom—a culmination of thousands of years of experience, knowledge, reason, and faith. The Declaration of Independence is a remarkable societal proclamation of human rights, brilliant in its insight, clarity, and conciseness. The Constitution of the United States is an extraordinary matrix of governmental limits, checks, balances, and divisions, intended to secure for posterity the individual's sovereignty as proclaimed in the Declaration.

This is the grand heritage to which every American citizen is born. It has been characterized as "the American Dream," "the American experiment," and "American exceptionalism." The country has been called "the Land of Opportunity," "the Land of Milk and Honey," and "a Shining City on a Hill." It seems unimaginable that a people so endowed by Providence, and the beneficiaries of such unparalleled human excellence, would choose or tolerate a course that ensures their own decline and enslavement, for a government unleashed on the civil society is a government that destroys the nature of man.

On September 17, 1787, at the conclusion of the Constitutional Convention in Philadelphia, Delegate James Wilson, on behalf of his ailing colleague from Pennsylvania, Benjamin Franklin, read aloud Franklin's speech to the convention in favor of adopting the Constitution. Among other things, Franklin said that the Constitution "is likely to be well administered for a Course of Years, and can only end in Despotism as other Forms have done before it, when the People shall become corrupt as to need Despotic Government, being incapable of any other. . . ."[2]

Have we "become corrupt"? Are we in need of "despotic government"? It appears that some modern-day "leading lights" think so, as they press their fanatical utopianism. For example, Richard Stengel, managing editor of *Time* magazine, considers the Constitution a utopian expedient. He wrote, "If the Constitution was intended to limit the federal government, it sure doesn't say so. . . . The framers weren't afraid of a little messiness. Which is another reason we shouldn't be so delicate about changing the Constitution or reinterpreting it."[3] It is beyond dispute that the Framers sought to limit the scope of federal power and that the Constitution does so. Moreover, constitutional change was not left to the masterminds but deliberately made difficult to ensure the broad participation and consent of the body politic.

Richard Cohen, a columnist for the *Washington Post*, explained that the Constitution is an amazing document, as long as it is mostly ignored, particularly the limits it imposes on the federal government. He wrote, "This fatuous infatuation with the Constitution, particularly the 10th Amendment, is clearly the work of witches, wiccans, and wackos. It has nothing to do with America's real problems and, if taken too seriously, would cause an economic and political calamity. The Constitution is a wonderful document, quite miraculous actually, but only because it has been wisely adapted to changing times. To adhere to the very word of its every clause hardly is respectful to the Founding Fathers. They were revolutionaries who embraced change. That's how we got here."[4] Of course, without the promise of the Tenth Amendment, the Constitution would not have been ratified, since the states insisted on retaining most of their sovereignty. Furthermore, the Framers clearly did not embrace the utopian change demanded by its modern adherents.

Lest we ignore history, the no-less-eminent American revolutionary and founder Thomas Jefferson explained, "On every question of construction, carry ourselves back to the time when the constitution was adopted, recollect the spirit manifested in the debates, and instead of trying what meaning may be squeezed out of the text, or invented against it, conform to the probable one in which it was passed."[5]

Thomas L. Friedman, a columnist for the *New York Times* and three-time Pulitzer Prize recipient, is even more forthright in his dismissal of constitutional republicanism and advocacy for utopian tyranny. Complaining of the slowness of American society in adopting sweeping utopian policies, he wrote, "There is only one thing worse than one-party autocracy, and that is one-party democracy, which is what we have in America today. One-party autocracy certainly has its drawbacks. But when it is led by a reasonably enlightened group of people, as China is today, it can also have great advantages. That one party can just impose the politically difficult but critically important policies needed to move a society forward in the 21st century."[6] Of course, China remains a police state, where civil liberties are nonexistent, despite its experiment with government-managed pseudo-capitalism. Friedman's declaration underscores not only the necessary intolerance utopians have for constitutionalism, but their infatuation with totalitarianism.

It is neither prudential nor virtuous to downplay or dismiss the obvious—that America has already transformed into *Ameritopia*. The centralization and consolidation of power in a political class that insulates its agenda in entrenched experts and administrators, whose authority is also self-perpetuating, is apparent all around us and growing more formidable. The issue is whether the ongoing transformation can be restrained and then reversed, or whether it will continue with increasing zeal, passing from a soft tyranny to something more oppressive. Hayek observed that "priding itself on having built its world as if it had designed it, and blaming itself for not having designed it better, humankind is now to set out to do just that. The aim . . . is no less than to effect a complete redesigning of our traditional morals, law, and language, and on this basis to stamp out the older order and supposedly inexorable, unjustifiable conditions that prevent the institution of reason, fulfillment, true freedom, and justice."[7] But the outcome of this adventurism, if not effectively stunted, is not in doubt.

In the end, can mankind stave off the powerful and dark forces of utopian tyranny? While John Locke was surely right about man's nature and the civil society, he was also right about that which threatens them. Locke, Montesquieu, many of the philosophers of the European Enlightenment, and the Founders, among others, knew that the history of organized government is mostly a history of a relative few and perfidious men co-opting, coercing, and eventually repressing the many through the centralization and consolidation of authority.

Ironically and tragically, it seems that liberty and the constitution established to preserve it are not only essential to the individual's well-being and happiness, but also an opportunity for the devious to exploit them and connive against them. Man has yet to devise a lasting institutional answer to this puzzle. The best that can be said is that all that really stands between the individual and tyranny is a resolute and sober people. It is the people, after all, around whom the civil society has grown and governmental institutions have been established. At last, the people are responsible for upholding the civil society and republican government, to which their fate is moored.

The essential question is whether, in America, the people's psychology has been so successfully warped, the individual's spirit so thoroughly trounced, and the civil society's institutions so effectively overwhelmed that revival is possible. Have too many among us already surrendered or been conquered? Can the people overcome the constant and relentless influences of ideological indoctrination, economic manipulation, and administrative coerciveness, or have they become hopelessly entangled in and dependent on a ubiquitous federal government? Have the Pavlovian appeals to radical egalitarianism, and the fomenting of jealousy and faction through class warfare and collectivism, conditioned the people to accept or even demand compulsory uniformity as just and righteous? Is it accepted as legitimate and routine that the government has sufficient license to act whenever it claims to do so for the good of the people and against the selfishness of the individual?

No society is guaranteed perpetual existence. But I have to believe that the American people are not ready for servitude, for if this is our destiny, and the destiny of our children, I cannot conceive that any people, now or in the future, will successfully resist it for long. I have to believe that this generation of Americans will not condemn future generations to centuries of misery and darkness.

The Tea Party movement is a hopeful sign. Its members come from all walks of life and every corner of the country. These citizens have the spirit and enthusiasm of the Founding Fathers, proclaim the principles of individual liberty and rights in the Declaration, and insist on the federal government's compliance with the Constitution's limits. This explains the utopian fury against them. They are astutely aware of the peril of the moment. But there are also the Pollyannas and blissfully indifferent citizens who must be roused and enlisted lest the civil society continue to unravel and eventually dissolve, and the despotism long feared take firm hold.

Upon taking the oath of office on January 20, 1981, in his first inaugural address President Ronald Reagan told the American people:

> *If we look to the answer as to why for so many years we achieved so much, prospered as no other people on earth, it was because here in this land we unleashed the energy and individual genius of man to a greater extent than has ever been done before. Freedom and the dignity of the individual have been more available and assured here than in any other place on earth. The price for this freedom at times has been high, but we have never been unwilling to pay that price. It is no coincidence that our present*

troubles parallel and are proportionate to the intervention and intrusion in our lives that result from unnecessary and excessive growth of government. It is time for us to realize that we are too great a nation to limit ourselves to small dreams. We're not, as some would have us believe, doomed to an inevitable decline. I do not believe in a fate that will fall on us no matter what we do. I do believe in a fate that will fall on us if we do nothing.

So, my fellow countrymen, which do we choose—*Ameritopia* or America?

NOTES

INTRODUCTION

1. Joseph Story, "The Value and Importance of Legal Studies," *The Miscellaneous Writings of Joseph Story*, William Story, ed. (Boston: Little, Brown, 1852), 513.
2. Abraham Lincoln, "Address Before the Young Men's Lyceum of Springfield, IL," *Complete Works of Abraham Lincoln*, John G. Nicolay and John Hay, eds., vol. 1 (New York: Century, 1894), 9.
3. Ronald Reagan, "Encroaching Control (The Peril of Ever Expanding Government)," *A Time for Choosing: The Speeches of Ronald Reagan 1961–1982*, Alfred A. Baltizer and Gerald M. Bonetto, eds. (Chicago: Regnery, 1983), 38.

1. THE TYRANNY OF UTOPIA

1. My references to utopianism are short for political utopianism.
2. Karl Popper, *The Poverty of Historicism* (London and New York: Routledge Classics, 2010), 43.

249

3. Ibid., 33–34.

4. Edmund Burke, *Reflections on the Revolution in France* (London: Seeley, 1872), 93.

5. Eric Hoffer, *The True Believer: Thoughts on the Nature of Mass Movements* (New York: Harper Perennial, 2010), 11.

6. Mark R. Levin, *Liberty and Tyranny: A Conservative Manifesto* (New York: Threshold Editions, 2009).

7. Alexis de Tocqueville, *Democracy in America*, vol. 2 (New York: Knopf Everyman's Edition, 1994), 87. Subsequent references to this work will be to (Volume, Page).

8. It is also important not to conflate the inability of people to redress radical egalitarianism with their acceptance of it.

9. Friedrich Hayek, *The Constitution of Liberty* (Chicago: University of Chicago Press, 1960), 85.

10. Levin, *Liberty and Tyranny*, 16–17.

11. See ibid., citing Adam Smith, *An Inquiry into the Nature and Causes of the Wealth of Nations* (New York: Collier, 1937).

12. Popper, *The Poverty of Historicism*, 73.

13. Whether recourse to violence builds into a popular uprising and whether the utopia survives depends on the nature of the utopia and myriad factors and events that are not the subject of this book.

14. Frédéric Bastiat, *The Law* (New York: Quality Books, 1998), 32–33.

15. Thomas Jefferson, *Notes on the State of Virginia* (New York: Literary Classics, 1984), 211.

16. Raymond Aron, *The Opium of the Intellectuals* (New Brunswick: Transaction, 2007), xiii–xiv.

17. Joseph Schumpeter, *Capitalism, Socialism, and Democracy* (New York: Harper, 1976), 153–54.

18. Bastiat, *The Law*, 4–5.

19. Popper, *The Poverty of Historicism*, 43.

20. F. A. Hayek, *The Fatal Conceit: The Errors of Socialism*, W. W. Bartley III, ed. (Chicago: University of Chicago Press, 1991), 152–53.

21. Levin, *Liberty and Tyranny*, 3–4.

22. James Madison, Alexander Hamilton, and John Jay, *The Federalist Papers* (New York: Penguin, 1987).

23. Ibid.

24. Stuart Taylor Jr., "Marshall Sounds Critical Note on Bicentennial," *New York Times*, May 7, 1987, as quoted in Mark R. Levin, *Men in Black: How the Supreme Court Is Destroying America* (Washington, D.C.: Regnery, 2004), 9.

25. Ibid.

26. Speech at Lewistown, Illinois, Aug. 17, 1858, *The Collected Works of Abraham Lincoln*, vol. 2 (New Brunswick: Rutgers University Press, 1953), 546–47.

27. Levin, *Liberty and Tyranny*, 4, quoting Alexis de Toqueville, *Democracy in America* (New York: Penguin, 2003).

2. Plato's *Republic* and the Perfect Society

1. Plato, *Republic* (New York: Barnes & Noble Classics, 2004). All references to *Republic* are to the commonly accepted line numbering system used in this as well as most other translations.

2. Although the ruling class comes from the guardian population, for purposes of this discussion they will be used interchangeably.

3. Donald J. Zeyl, ed., *Encyclopedia of Classical Philosophy* (London: Routledge, 1947), 400. See Aristotle, *Metaphysics*.

4. *Encyclopedia of Classical Philosophy*, 404.

5. See F. C. Copleston, ed., *A History of Philosophy*, vol. 1 (New York: Image Books, 1985), 232–33.

6. Ibid.

7. Karl R. Popper, *The Open Society and its Enemies*, vol. 1, *Plato* (Princeton: Princeton University Press, 1971), 102.

8. Raymond H. Anderson, "Ayatollah Ruhollah Khomani, 89, Relentless Founder of Iran's Islamic Republic," *New York Times*, June 5, 1989, http://www.nytimes.com/1989/06/05/world/ ayatollah-ruhollah-khomeini-89–relentless-founder-of-iran-s -islamic-republic.html?pagewanted=all&src=pm (July 16, 2011).

9. Popper, *Plato*, 199–200.

3. Thomas More's *Utopia* and Radical Egalitarianism

1. Thomas More, *Utopia*. First published in Antwerp, 1516, in Latin. The first English language translation, by Ralph Robinson, was published in 1551. The edition used herein was edited by Wayne A. Rebhorn (New York: Barnes and Noble Classics, 2005). Unless otherwise noted, all page references in this chapter are to *Utopia*.

4. Thomas Hobbes's *Leviathan* and the All-Powerful State

1. Thomas Hobbes, *Leviathan*, Edwin Curley, ed. (Indianapolis: Hackett, 1994). Subsequent references to this work will be to page number.

5. Karl Marx's *Communist Manifesto* and the Class Struggle

1. Karl Marx and Friedrich Engels, *The Communist Manifesto* (London: SoHo, 2010). Subsequent references to this work are to (Page).

2. Karl R. Popper, *The Open Society and Its Enemies*, vol. 2, *Hegel and Marx* (Princeton: Princeton University Press, 1971), 83 (emphasis in original).

3. Raymond Aron, *The Opium of the Intellectuals* (New Brunswick: Transaction, 2007), 339.

4. Mark R. Levin, *Liberty and Tyranny: A Conservative Manifesto* (New York: Threshold Editions, 2009), 65–66.

5. "America Runs on Small Chamber," *Main Street Chamber*, Sept. 29, 2010, http://www.mainstreetchamber-mn.org/2010/09/29/ameria-runs-on-small-business-2/ (July 16, 2011).

6. Aron, *The Opium of the Intellectuals*, 343.

6. John Locke and the Nature of Man

1. John Locke, *An Essay Concerning Human Understanding* (Oxford: Oxford University Press, 2008). Subsequent references to this work will be to (Book, Chapter, Section).

2. John Locke, *The Second Treatise of Government* (New York: Barnes & Noble, 2004). Subsequent references to this work will be to (Chapter, Section).

7. The Influence of Locke on the Founders

1. Livingston was one of the delegates who did not sign the Declaration as he believed, among other things, that reconciliation with Britain was still possible.

2. John Locke, *Two Treatises of Government*, Peter Laslett, ed. (Cambridge: Cambridge University Press, 2010). Subsequent references to this work will be to (Chapter, Section).

3. Thomas Jefferson's "original rough draught" of the Declaration of Independence, http://www.princeton.edu/~tjpapers/declaration/declaration.html (July 13, 2011).

4. James Madison, "Property," *National Gazette*, March 29, 1792, http://teachingamericanhistory.org/library/index.asp?document=600 (July 13, 2011).

5. William Blackstone, *Commentaries on the Laws of England*, http://avalon.law.yale.edu/18th_century/blackstone_intro.asp#2 (July 13, 2011).

6. Madison, "Property."

7. Jeffrey M. Gaba, "John Locke and the Meaning of the Takings Clause," 72 *Missouri Law Review* 525, 527 n.4 (2007) citing William Michael Treanor, "The Origins and Original Significance of the Just Compensation Clause of the Fifth Amendment," 94 *Yale Law Journal* 694, 708–12 (1985).

8. U.S. Constitution, Fifth Amendment.

9. Bernard Bailyn, *The Ideological Origins of the American Revolution* (Cambridge: Harvard University Press, 1992), 27.

8. CHARLES DE MONTESQUIEU AND
REPUBLICAN GOVERNMENT

1. Charles Montesquieu, *The Spirit of the Laws*, Anne M. Cohler, Basia C. Miller, and Harold S. Stone, eds. (Cambridge: Cambridge University Press, 2009) (Part 1, Book 1, Chapter 2). Subsequent references to this work will be to (Part, Book, Chapter).

9. THE INFLUENCE OF MONTESQUIEU ON THE FRAMERS

1. Donald S. Lutz, *The Origins of American Constitutionalism* (Baton Rouge: Louisiana State University Press, 1988), 143.
2. John R. Vile, *The Constitutional Convention of 1787: A Comprehensive Encyclopedia of America's Founding*, vol. 1 (Santa Barbara: ABC-CLIO, 2005), 495.
3. Ibid., citing Max Farrand, ed., *The Records of the Federal Convention*, vol. 1 (New Haven: Yale University Press, 1937), 71.
4. Ibid., citing Farrand, I, 308.
5. Ibid., citing Farrand, I, 391.
6. Ibid., citing Farrand, I, 485.
7. Ibid., citing Farrand, II, 34.
8. Ibid., citing Farrand, II, 530.
9. Ibid., citing Farrand, I, 580.
10. Ibid., citing Forrest McDonald, *Novus Ordo Seclorum: The Intellectual Origins of the Constitution* (Lawrence: University Press of Kansas, 1985), 233.
11. James Madison, Alexander Hamilton, and John Jay, *The Federalist Papers* (New York: Penguin, 1987).
12. Ibid.

13. David Wootton, ed., *The Essential Federalist and Anti-Federalist Papers* (Indianapolis: Hackett, 2003), 99.

14. Ibid., 105.

15. Ibid., 11–12.

16. Ibid., 13.

17. Ibid., 15.

18. Herbert J. Storing, ed., *The Complete Anti-Federalist*, vol. 1, ch. 4, doc. 16 (Cato, no. 3) (Chicago: University of Chicago Press, 1981).

19. Madison, Hamilton, and Jay, *The Federalist Papers*.

20. Ibid.

21. Ibid.

22. Ibid.

23. Ibid.

24. U.S. Constitution, Tenth Amendment. Compare with Articles of Confederation, Article II: "Each state retains its sovereignty, freedom, and independence, and every power, jurisdiction, and right, which is not by this Confederation expressly delegated to the United States in Congress assembled."

25. U.S. Constitution, Ninth Amendment.

26. Kurt T. Lash, "The Lost Original Meaning of the Ninth Amendment," 83 *Texas Law Review* 331, 392 (2004).

27. Ibid., quoting James Madison, *Writings*, Jack N. Rakove, ed. (New York: Library of America, 1999), 489.

28. Ibid., quoting *Gazette of the United States* (Philadelphia), Feb. 23, 1791, reprinted in *Documentary History of the First Federal Congress, 1789–1791*, William Charles diGiacomantonio et al., eds., vol. 14 (Baltimore: Johns Hopkins University Press, 1996), 367.

29. James Madison, *Notes of Debates in the Federal Convention of 1787* (Athens, OH: Ohio University Press, 1985), 7.

10. ALEXIS DE TOCQUEVILLE AND *DEMOCRACY IN AMERICA*

1. Alexis de Tocqueville, *Democracy in America*, vol. I (New York: Knopf, 1994), 46. Subsequent references to this work will be to (Volume, Page).

11. POST-CONSTITUTIONAL AMERICA

1. Christopher Collier and James Lincoln Collier, *Decision in Philadelphia: The Constitutional Convention of 1787* (New York: Ballantine, 2007), 250.
2. James Madison, Alexander Hamilton, and John Jay, *The Federalist Papers* (New York: Penguin, 1987).
3. Ibid.
4. Woodrow Wilson, *Constitutional Government in the United States* (New York: Columbia University Press, 1908), 16.
5. Ibid., 4–5.
6. Ibid., 54.
7. Ibid., 56.
8. Ibid., 56–57.
9. Ibid., 70.
10. Ibid., 167.
11. Ibid., 167–68.
12. Ibid., 172.
13. Ibid., 193.

14. Ibid., 178.

15. Ibid.

16. Ibid., 189.

17. Ibid., 192.

18. Franklin D. Roosevelt, *Whither Bound?* (Boston: Houghton Mifflin, 1926), 14–16.

19. Ibid., 19–20.

20. Levin, *Liberty and Tyranny.*

21. Franklin D. Roosevelt, "State of the Union Message to Congress," Jan. 11, 1944, http://www.fdrlibrary.marist.edu/archives/address_text.html (July 14, 2011).

22. Ibid.

23. Ibid.

24. Cass R. Sunstein, *The Second Bill of Rights: FDR's Unfinished Revolution and Why We Need It More than Ever* (New York: Basic Books, 2004), 232–33.

25. Ibid., 234.

26. 1936 Constitution of the USSR, http://www.departments.bucknell.edu/russian/const/36cons04.html#chap10 (July 14, 2011).

27. Whittaker Chambers, *Witness* (Washington, D.C.: Gateway, 2002), 472.

28. http://www.youtube.com/watch?v=_cqN4NIEtOY (July 14, 2011).

12. AMERITOPIA

1. F. A. Hayek, *The Fatal Conceit: The Errors of Socialism*, W. W. Bartley III, ed. (Chicago: University of Chicago Press, 1991), 14.

2. Kyle Mundry, "Individual Income Tax Rates and Shares," Internal Revenue Service, 2008, IRS Bulletin http://www.irs.gov/pub/irs-soi/11intr08winbul.pdf (July 17, 2011), 31.

3. "Historical Tables, Budget of the U.S. Government, Fiscal Year 2011," U.S. Government Printing Office, http://www.gpoaccess .gov/usbudget/fy11/pdf/hist.pdf (July 17, 2011).

4. "The Moment of Truth," National Commission on Fiscal Responsibility and Reform, http://www.fiscalcommission.gov/sites/ fiscalcommission.gov/files/documents/TheMomentofTruth12_ 1_2010.pdf (July 17, 2011).

5. "CBO's 2011 Long-Term Budget Outlook," CBO REPORT, Congressional Budget Office, June 2011.

6. National Commission, "The Moment of Truth."

7. CBO 2011 Long-Term Budget Outlook.

8. Dennis Cauchon, "U.S. funding for future promises lags by trillions," USA Today, June 6, 2011, http://www.usatoday.com/news/ washington/2011–06–06–us-owes-62–trillion-in-debt_n.htm (July 18, 2011).

9. Ibid.

10. Dennis Cauchon, "Federal workers earning double their private counterparts," USA Today, Aug. 13, 2010, http://www.usatoday .com/money/economy/income/2010–08–10–1Afedpay10_ST _N.htm (July 14, 2011).

11. Iain Murray, "There Is No 'Regulation Day' to Remind Us How Much They Cost," National Review, The Corner, April 18, 2011, http:// www.nationalreview.com/corner/264984/there-no-regulation-day -remind-us-how-much-they-cost-iain-murray (July 14, 2011).

12. Nicole V. Crain and W. Mark Crain, "The Regulation Tax Keeps Growing," Wall Street Journal, Sept. 27, 2010, http://online.wsj .com/article/SB10001424052748703860104575508122499819564.html (July 14, 2011).

13. Brian Walsh, "Overcriminalization: An Explosion of Federal Criminal Law," Heritage Foundation, April 27, 2011, http://www

.heritage.org/research/factsheets/2011/04/overcriminalization
-an-explosion-of-federal-criminal-law (July 14, 2011).

14. See www.epa.gov/oar/oaqps/; www.epa.gov/owow/wetlands/regs/
index.html; http://endangered.fws.gov/policies/index.html; www
.epa.gov/opptintr/lead/fslbp.htm; www.epa.gov/opptintr/pcb; and
www.achp.gov/regs.html.

15. U.S. Army Corps of Engineers, "Recognizing Wetlands," http://
www.nao.usace.army.mil/technical%20services/Regulatory%20
branch/RBwetlands.asp (July 14, 2011).

16. See Consumer Product Safety Act, 15 U.S.C. Sections 2051–
2089 (2008).

17. Murray Weidenbaum, "Government Regulation of the Automobile," Heartland Institute, Jan. 1, 1999, http://www.heartland
.org/policybot/results/381/Government_Regulation_of_the_
Automobile.html (July 14, 2011).

18. Randal O'Toole, "Obama's Fuel-Economy Standards," Cato Institute, May 20, 2009, http://www.cato-at-liberty.org/obamas-fuel
-economy-standards/ (July 14, 2011).

19. "Obama unveils sharp increase in auto fuel economy," Reuters,
July 29, 2011, http://www.reuters.com/article/2011/07/29/us
-usa-autos-standards-idUSTRE76S4AR20110729 (October 10,
2011).

20. David Shepardson, "Study: Fuel rules to hike car costs," *Detroit
News*, June 15, 2011, http://www.detnews.com/article/20110615/
AUTO01/106150378/1148/Study--Fuel-rules-to-hike-car-costs
(July 14, 2011).

21. Ran Balis, "CAFÉ Standards Kill: Congress' Regulatory Solution
to Foreign Oil Dependence Comes at a Steep Price," National
Center for Public Policy Research, National Policy Analysis

546, July 2006, http://www.nationalcenterorg/NPA546CAFE Standards.html (July 14, 2011).

22. 40 CFR 85, 86, 600 & 49 CER 575. See also Fact Sheet: New Fuel Economy and Environment Labels for a New Generation of Vehicles, http://www.afdc.energy.gov/afdc/ethanol/incentives_laws_federal.html?print.

23. Ibid.

24. Tim Devaney, "Petroleum leader decries 'extreme' regs," *Washington Times*, July 12, 2011, http://www.washingtontimes.com/news/2011/jul/12/petroleum-leader-decries-extreme-regulations/ (July 14, 2011).

25. 16 CFR 306.5.

26. 40 CFR 80.1100–80.1167. See also U.S. Department of Energy, Alternative Fuels and Advanced Vehicles Data Center, http://www.afdc.energy.gov/afdc/ethanol/incentives_laws_federal.html?print (July 16, 2011).

27. 40 CFR 63.11116.

28. 16 CFR 306.10.

29. 29 CFR 1910.263(k)(2)(i).

30. See 9 CFR Part 317.

31. 21 CFR 174–90.

32. http://www.ftc.gov/os/2011/04/110428foodmarketproposedguide.pdf.

33. Ibid.

34. Education and the Workforce Committee, Committee Statements, "Duncan Statement: Hearing on 'Examining the Cost of Federal Overreach into School Meals,'" May 13, 2011, http://edworkforce.house.gov/News/DocumentSingle.aspx?DocumentID=241182 (July 14, 2011); "Goodbye to Bake Sales? Nutri-

tion Bill Subjects School Fundraisers to New Regs," Fox News, Dec. 8, 2010, http://www.foxnews.com/politics/2010/12/08/ goodbye-bake-sales-nutrition-subjects-school-fundraisers-new -regs/ (July 14, 2011).

35. Sheryl Gay Stolberg and William Neuman, "Restaurant Nutrition Draws Focus of First Lady," New York Times, Feb. 6, 2011.

36. Patient Protection and Affordable Care Act, Pub. L. No. 111–148, Section 4205, 124 Stat. 119 (2010).

37. Richard Verrier, "What's in the Popcorn? Cinemas Would Rather Not Have to Say," Los Angeles Times, March 23, 2011.

38. See Victor Davis Hanson, "The Department of Food Subsidies," National Review, June 23, 2011, http://www.nationalreview.com/ articles/270233/department-food-subsidies-victor-davis-hanson (July 14, 2011).

39. Americans with Disabilities Act, 42 U.S.C. Section 12,101 et seq.

40. PPACA, Section 4205.

41. Henry Rogers Seager, Social Insurance: A Program of Social Reform (New York: Macmillan, 1910).

42. Levin, Liberty and Tyranny, 96.

43. Seager, Social Insurance, 1–2.

44. Ibid., 3.

45. Ibid., 5.

46. Ibid., 118.

47. Ibid., 150–51.

48. Ibid., 151–61.

49. Ibid., 161–62.

50. Ibid., 162.

51. Ibid., 168.

52. Ibid., 175.

53. Charlotte A. Twight, *Dependent on D.C.: The Rise of Federal Control Over the Lives of Ordinary Americans* (New York: Palgrave, 2002), 62.

54. Ibid.

55. Levin, *Liberty and Tyranny*, 98, citing Arthur Schlesinger Jr., *The Coming of the New Deal* (Boston: Houghton Mifflin, 1959), 308.

56. Twight, *Dependent on D.C.*, 76.

57. The 2011 Annual Report of the Board of Trustees, Federal Old Age and Survivors Insurance and Federal Disability Insurance Trust Fund (Washington, D.C.: U.S. Government Printing Office, June 2011), 2.

58. Twight, *Dependent on D.C.*, 199.

59. Levin, *Liberty and Tyranny*, 102, citing Lyndon B. Johnson, "Remarks with President Truman at the Signing in Independence of the Medicare Bill," July 30, 1965, Lyndon Baines Johnson Library and Museum, http://www.lbjlib.utexas.edu/Johnson/archives.hom/speeches.hom/650730.asp (July 14, 2010).

60. Ibid.

61. Ibid., 103, citing Larry DeWitt, "The Medicare Program as a Capstone to the Great Society—Recent Revelations in the LBJ White House Tapes," citing White House tape WH6503.11, Lyndon Baines Johnson Library and Museum, May 2003, http//www.larrydewitt.net/Essays/MedicareDaddy.htm.

62. The 2011 Annual Report of the Boards of Trustees of the Federal Hospital Insurance and Federal Supplementary Medical Insurance Trust Funds (Washington, D.C.: U.S. Government Printing Office, May 2011), 4.

63. Congressional Budget Office, *The Budget and Economic Outlook: Fiscal Years 2010 to 2020.*

64. "Financial Condition of Social Security," Peter G. Peterson Foundation, June 6, 2011, http://www.pgpf.org/Issues/Fiscal-Outlook/2011/06/The-Financial-Condition-of-Social-Security.aspx?p=1 (July 14, 2011).

65. Richard S. Foster, "Statement of Actuarial Opinion," 2011 Federal Hospital Insurance Trustees Report, 266.

66. 2011 Federal Hospital Insurance Trustees Report, 52.

67. Franklin D. Roosevelt, "State of the Union Message to Congress," Jan. 11, 1944, http://www.fdrlibrary.marist.edu/archives/address_text.html (July 14, 2011).

68. Levin, *Liberty and Tyranny*, 102, citing Harry Truman, "Annual Message to the Congress on the State of the Union," January 7, 1948, http://www.c-span.org/executive/transcript.asp?cat=bush_admin&year=1948.

69. Frank Newport, "Americans Expect Health Bill to Mainly Help Poor, Uninsured," Gallup, March 19, 2010, http://www.gallup.com/poll/126812/Americans-Expect-Health-Bill-Mainly-Help-Poor-Uninsured.aspx?version=print (July 14, 2011).

70. Peter Roff, "Pelosi: Pass Health Reform So You Can Find Out What's In It," *U.S. News & World Report*, Politics blog, March 9, 2010, http://www.usnews.com/opinion/blogs/peter-roff/2010/03/09/pelosi-pass-health-reform-so-you-can-find-out-whats-in-it (July 14, 2011).

71. Thomas Jefferson, "Letter to James Madison," *The Debate on the Constitution* (New York: Library of America, 1993), 213.

72. Shailagh Murray, "Bill Clinton urges Senate Democrats to quickly pass health-care reform," *Washington Post*, Nov. 11, 2009, http://www.washingtonpost.com/wp-dyn/content/article/2009/11/10/AR2009111017413.html (July 14, 2011).

73. Barack Obama, "Remarks By the President at the Annual Conference of the American Medical Association," June 15, 2009, http://www.whitehouse.gov/the-press-office/remarks-president-annual-conference-american-medical-association (July 14, 2011).

74. Shubham Singhal, Jeris Stueland, and Drew Ungerman, "How U.S. health care reform will affect employee benefits," *McKinsey Quarterly*, June 2011, http://www.mckinseyquarterly.com/How_US_health_care_reform_will_affect_employee_benefits_2813 (July 14, 2011).

75. Obama, "AMA Remarks."

76. Ibid.

77. Martin Feldstein, "ObamaCare Is All About Rationing," *Wall Street Journal*, August 18, 2009, http://online.wsj.com/article/SB10001424052970204683204574358233780260914.html (July 14, 2011).

78. "Editorial: ObamaCare's Costs Just Keep Rising," *Investors Business Daily*, April 20, 2011, http://www.investors.com/NewsAndAnalysis/Article/569810/201104201922/ObamaCares-Costs-Are-Rising.aspx (July 14, 2011).

79. "Editorial: Obamacare's casualties: 800,000 jobs," *Washington Times*, Feb. 11, 2011, http://www.washingtontimes.com/news/2011/feb/11/obamacares-casualties-800000-jobs/ (July 14, 2011).

80. Douglas W. Emendorf, Director, Congressional Budget Office, "Letter to Honorable Jerry Lewis," May 11, 2010, http://www.cbo.gov/ftpdocs/114xx/doc11490/LewisLtr_HR3590.pdf (July 14, 2011).

81. http://www.youtube.com/watch?v=M7Ofgb4PDwY.

82. Benjamin Domenech, "CMS Nominee Donald Berwick's Radical Agenda," Heartland Institute, May 12, 2010, http://www.heart

land.org/healthpolicy-news.org/article/27630/CMS_Nominee_
Donald_Berwicks_Radical_Agenda.html (July 14, 2011).

83. http://www.youtube.com/watch?v=OoqI5PSRcXM.

84. Conn Carroll, "Morning Bell: Obamacare's Failed First Year," Heritage Foundation, The Foundry blog, March 23, 2011, http://blog.heritage.org/2011/03/23/morning-bell-obamacares-failed-first-year/ (July 14, 2011).

85. Chris Jaarda, "ObamaCare's Advanced Appropriations Put Government Takeover on Auto-Pilot," American Healthcare Education Coalition, Nov. 30, 2010, http://healthcare-coalition.org/_blog/Prescription_For_Disaster/post/ObamaCare%27s_Advanced_Appropriations_Put_Gov%27t_Takeover_on_Auto-Pilot/ (July 14, 2011).

86. Peter Ferrara, "The Obamacare Disaster: An Appraisal of the Patient Protection and Affordable Care Act," Heartland Policy Study #128, Heartland Institute, Chicago, 2010, v.

87. Curtis W. Copeland, "New Entities Created Pursuant to the Patient Protection and Affordable Care Act," Congressional Research Service, July 8, 2010, 2.

88. PPACA, Section 1501.

89. U.S. Constitution, Art. I, Section 6.

Epilogue

1. David Miller, *Popper Selections* (Princeton: Princeton University Press, 1985), 340.

2. Benjamin Franklin, *Writings* (New York: Penguin, 1997), 1140.

3. Richard Stengel, "One Document, Under Siege," *Time*, June 23, 2011, http://www.time.com/time/nation/article/0,8599,2079445,00.html (July 17, 2011).

4. Richard Cohen, "Republicans Under Spell," *Washington Post*, Sept. 21, 2010, http://www.washingtonpost.com/wp-dyn/content/article/2010/09/20/AR2010092004256.html (July 17, 2011).

5. Thomas Jefferson, "The Usurpation of Supreme Court," (June 12, 1823, Letter to William Johnson), *The Complete Jefferson*, Saul K. Padover, ed. (New York: Duell, Sloan & Pearce, 1943) 322.

6. Thomas Friedman, "Our One-Party Democracy," *New York Times*, Sept. 8, 2009, http://www.nytimes.com/2009/09/09/opinion/09friedman.html (July 17, 2011).

7. Hayek, *Fatal Conceit*, 167.

ACKNOWLEDGMENTS

WRITING A BOOK, ESPECIALLY this book, is a solitary and time-consuming undertaking. A special thank-you is owed my amazing children, Lauren and Chase, for their love and understanding. I adore them and could not be more proud of them. It is for them, and their generation, that I wrote this book. And to Kendall, the most decent person I have ever known.

Thank you to my wonderful parents, Jack and Norma, who sacrificed so my brothers and I might succeed and encouraged me throughout my life with their love, wisdom, and guidance. They are my heroes. I can never repay them. And there are no better and more loyal brothers than Douglas and Robert, to whom I am forever grateful and for whom I am deeply blessed.

I want to thank my longtime and dear friend Eric Christensen for his invaluable insight, counsel, and research assistance, as well as my friends and outstanding colleagues at Landmark Legal Foundation—Richard Hutchison, Robert Levin, Michael O'Neill, and Matthew Forys—for their excellent research assistance. Thanks to Professor Thomas West for his kind response to an inquiry respecting the Declaration of Independence.

This is the third book in which my editor, Mitchell Ivers of Simon & Schuster, has provided superb input. Thanks to him and my publisher, Louise Burke, for their enthusiasm for this project. And thanks to my friend and lawyer, David Limbaugh, for his wise advice and many kindnesses, and Rush Limbaugh and Sean Hannity for their friendship, generosity, and support.

Finally, to my fellow Americans—you have sacrificed so much for the betterment of mankind, for which you are owed the world's gratitude. But we must now muster the same strength, courage, and wisdom to confront the perils we face at home today. We cannot put it off to some future date. Our generation is duty-bound to the next generation to preserve this great republic, just as our forefathers were duty-bound to us. The day is late and the hour is now.

In memory of
Pepsi, Griffen, and Sprite Levin

Thank you for all the joy and happiness.